T0047596

IT ALL
ADDS UP

DEVON KENNARD

IT ALL ADDS UP

Designing Your Game Plan
for Financial Success

HARPERCOLLINS
LEADERSHIP

AN IMPRINT OF HARPERCOLLINS

© 2023 Devon Kennard

All rights reserved. No portion of this book may be reproduced, stored in a retrieval system, or transmitted in any form or by any means—electronic, mechanical, photocopy,
recording, scanning, or other—except for brief quotations in critical reviews or articles,
without the prior written permission of the publisher.

Published by HarperCollins Leadership, an imprint of HarperCollins Focus LLC.

Any internet addresses, phone numbers, or company or product information printed in
this book are offered as a resource and are not intended in any way to be or to imply an
endorsement by HarperCollins Leadership, nor does HarperCollins Leadership vouch for
the existence, content, or services of these sites, phone numbers, companies, or products
beyond the life of this book.

Book design by Aubrey Khan, Neuwirth & Associates, Inc.

ISBN 978-1-4002-3377-9 (eBook)
ISBN 978-1-4002-3376-2 (TP)

Library of Congress Control Number: 2023931447

Printed in the United States of America
23 24 25 26 27 LBC 5 4 3 2 1

This book is written as a source of information only. The information contained in this book should by no means be considered a substitute for the advice, decisions, or judgment of the reader's professional or financial advisors. All efforts have been made to ensure the accuracy of the information contained in this book as of the date published. The author and the publisher expressly disclaim responsibility for any adverse effects arising from the use or application of the information contained herein.

To my two daughters, Camryn Jae Kennard and Carsyn Jae Kennard. Long before you two were born I thought of one day having children. Just the thought of both of you has kept me focused and driven my entire life. I truthfully do not care what you decide to do for a living once you are older; what matters to me is what you do with what you got! Be the best *you* can be, baby girls. I promise that is enough!

I wrote this book with you guys in mind so I could pass along to you some of the best lessons I have learned up to this point in my life. I hope that you will take as much as you can and apply it to your own lives.

Daddy's love for you two is *eternal*!

CONTENTS

IT ALL ADDS UP

CHAPTER ONE

My Game Plan

Football is what I do. It's not who I am.

When I was a kid, my identity was simply "Devon the football player." It was *what* I did and *who* I was. My only goal back then was to make it to the NFL. I wanted to be just like my dad, Derek Kennard. An old photo of my dad and me in *Sports Illustrated* would show you why!

My dad, Derek Kennard, carrying me after winning with the
Dallas Cowboys against the Pittsburgh Steelers in Super Bowl XXX
Photo credit: Walter Iooss Jr./Sports Illustrated via Getty Images

I was four and a half years old at the time, sitting on his shoulders raising my arm victoriously in the air, taken minutes after he and his Dallas Cowboys teammates had beaten the Pittsburgh Steelers, 27–17, in Super Bowl XXX. That is one of the few moments I remember about my dad's NFL career, but I knew then I wanted to be just like him.

It wasn't much later that I drew up my first game plan. It looked something like this:

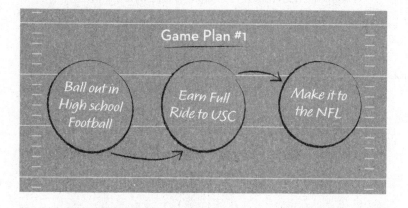

It looked simple enough: all I had to do was ball out in high school football, earn a college scholarship, ball out in college, and then get drafted into the NFL.

Fast-forward to my senior year at Desert Vista High School in Phoenix, Arizona. One Saturday I was watching the University of Southern California Trojans game, sitting on the couch, crying in a moment of self-pity, recuperating from knee surgery. It was done to repair a torn anterior cruciate ligament (ACL) that I had recently suffered in a game against Chandler High School.

The irony about my injury is that I got hurt playing out of my normal position, which is predominantly on defense. When one of our running backs nearly fumbled, and since it was a close game, our coach asked me if I wanted to go in for him. I had played some running back in short-yardage situations my whole career, so I said, "Hell, yeah," and I ran onto the field with no hesitation. And that's when I was injured. Devastating. It was also the last time I ever played on offense.

During a high school football game
Photo credit: Devon Kennard

From the moment I started playing football, I've always been a hard-working and talented athlete. After my freshman season, I was moved up to varsity—one of the few freshmen in Desert Vista High School history to get so promoted. That gave me a huge boost of confidence, motivating me all the more to work extra hard to become an immediate impact player at the varsity level.

The work ethic paid off. As a junior, I led the nation's high schoolers with 24.5 sacks, at the time the most ever in Arizona history. As a senior, and before my injury, I was selected as a US Army All-American, was a five-star recruit, and was ranked as a top-five recruit in the nation.

My talents and efforts were getting recognized long before my senior year. After both my sophomore and junior years, I was invited to USC to participate in the biggest summer college football camp on the West Coast, and it's fair to say I dominated playing defensive end/outside linebacker. All the big universities had expressed interest in me while I was still a sophomore. I vividly remember Pete Carroll, USC's legendary coach at the time, walking into my English class and wanting to talk to me—me!—about playing for the Trojans! It was surreal!

Coach Carroll wasn't the only one watching me. Alabama head coach Nick Saban, and Notre Dame's then coach Charlie Weis also met with me, among many others. It also worked in my favor that I was getting great grades—that was as important to me as it was to the coaches—and was excelling in football, putting me on track to get into a great college and one step closer to the NFL. *I just needed to stay healthy.*

On the fateful play, the Desert Vista quarterback called for a toss, received the snap, and quickly lateraled the ball to me. I grabbed it okay and took off, but one of Chandler's corners had already recognized the play; he beat the lead wide receiver to the edge and had the perfect angle to hit me low. Before I could brace myself, let alone make a cut to avoid him, he threw his entire body weight into my knee. I collapsed, threw off my helmet, and squirmed in pain. My brother, Derek Jr., also one of our coaches, ran onto the field with the trainers. As he would later tell me, he immediately knew something was seriously wrong with my knee.

An MRI broke the bad news: I had torn my ACL and needed season-ending surgery. My last year of playing high school football was over. An ACL tear, one of the most feared injuries for any athlete in any sport, has cut short the careers of many professional and amateur athletes. When I had first sat down on that couch to watch that USC game, I had already convinced myself that I would be one of them.

The entire foundation of who I was at the time was tethered to this game. Now I felt like my identity was gone and my game plan had been suddenly disrupted. I was no longer Devon the football player. Without football, or the uniform to wear with it, things changed for me. It's not that my homies didn't care about me, but the phone stopped ringing as much as it had been. Word of an injury to a top recruit spreads quickly in the world of coaches and recruiters.

So there I was, glued to the couch, sulking and whimpering. My parents really tried to help. They urged me to go to my school's homecoming dance to hang out with my friends, but they had rented a party bus and my knee wasn't yet strong enough to climb on or off it. My parents continued trying to persuade me, and it worked. I decided I would do it, that I would at least go to the dance, and told my friends I would meet them there—like I said, no party bus for me.

It was 7:30 p.m. when I arrived at the school gym, only to find that it was pretty much all freshmen cluttering the dance floor. I didn't want any part of that, obviously, so I hobbled to the boys' restroom as quickly as I could on my crutches, the idea being that I would kill time there. It was pitiful—future pro football star, sneaking off to the restroom after being spooked by a dance floor full of freshmen. Not a proud moment of my life.

About twenty minutes later, my friends arrived and essentially rescued me. I grabbed my crutches and went to join them in the hallway, where some of the girls were pointing at me and laughing. I didn't know what was so funny about a guy limping around with a torn ACL. I certainly couldn't figure out what the big joke was until one of my friends came running over to tell me,

"Bro, you got toilet paper hanging out of your pants."

Things had quickly gone from bad to worse. It didn't matter that all I had done was put down some paper on the toilet seat so I could sit down while waiting for my friends.

I can laugh about it now, but when something like this happens to you as a teenager and you're made the butt of jokes (no pun intended), it's super embarrassing. I went from being a popular man on campus to just being some injured football jock being laughed at for toilet paper hanging off his pants.

I didn't take it well. It was an all-time, ego-crushing blow for me. It was also the first time in my life that I wondered if I was ever going to make it pro. If I didn't, then what? This was a big aha moment for me, and I knew that something needed to change. It was also a great lesson for me, although it didn't seem so at the time.

The Parable of the Bags of Gold

I used my recovery time from surgery to build a better relationship with God. My faith had always been very important to me, but it had wavered some and it was time for me to start going back to church. It was at this time in church that I first heard of the parable of the bags of gold. It carried a message that has stayed with me to this day, and it goes like this:

A man going on a journey [calls] his servants and entrusts his wealth to them. To one he gave five bags of gold, to another two bags, and to another one bag, each according to his ability. Then he went on his journey. The man who had received five bags of gold went at once and put his money to work and gained five bags more. So also, the one with two bags of gold gained two more. But the man who had received one bag went off, dug a hole in the ground and hid his master's money.

After a long time, the master of those servants returned and settled accounts with them. The man who had received five bags of gold brought the other five. "Master," he said, "you entrusted me with five bags of gold. See, I have gained five more."

His master replied, "Well done, good and faithful servant! You have been faithful with a few things; I will put you in charge of many things. Come and share your master's happiness!"

The man with two bags of gold also came. "Master," he said, "you entrusted me with two bags of gold; see, I have gained two more."

His master replied, "Well done, good and faithful servant! You have been faithful with a few things; I will put you in charge of many things. Come and share your master's happiness!"

Then the man who had received one bag of gold came. "Master," he said, "I knew that you are a hard man, harvesting where you have not sown and gathering where you have not scattered seed. So I was afraid and went out and hid your gold in the ground. See, here is what belongs to you."

His master replied, "You wicked, lazy servant! So you knew that I harvest where I have not sown and gather where I have not scattered seed? Well then, you should have put my money on deposit with the bankers, so that when I returned I would have received it back with interest.

"So take the bag of gold from him and give it to the one who has ten bags. For whoever has will be given more, and they will have an abundance. Whoever does not have, even what they have will be taken from them. And throw that worthless servant outside, into the darkness, where there will be weeping and gnashing of teeth." (Matthew 25:14–30, New International Version)

I'm thankful that my recovery and return to church led me to this parable's valuable lesson: *You can't control what you're given. It's what you do with what you're given that matters.* It sucked being injured, but the parable showed me that I have been given many opportunities and blessings in my life that I needed to appreciate and maximize.

Until this point, my senior year in high school, I had suffered from tunnel vision—I had been focused only on getting into the NFL. Now I wanted more out of my life instead of just football success. Whether I returned to football or not, I didn't want to ever feel this useless again. Instead, I wanted to be like that first servant who turns five bags of gold into ten. I wanted to "flip the bag," in my own life, so to speak; but I also had a desire to help others to multiply their blessings.

Beyond the NFL

According to the National Football League Players Association (NFLPA), the average length of an NFL career is only 3.3 seasons.[1]

I didn't know that when I was in high school, but I did know that even if I made it to the NFL, my career wasn't going to last forever. The day would come when I would hang up my cleats, and then what? Start a career in sports broadcasting? Relax and travel the world? Own a business? I didn't know what my post-football career would be, but I started thinking about it as well as what would come after. Notice how that last part had not made it into my original game plan.

Thankfully, even with my injury and short senior season, college coaches still recognized my skills. I remained a top-ten recruit in the nation at my position with forty schools still recruiting me. Unbelievable! My dream of an NFL career was still alive.

For years, I had always known which school I wanted to play for, and by now you must know which one it is. I had fallen in love with the energy of USC's football program and wanted to chase excellence. And man, they were excellent! By the time I was a high school senior, the Trojans had won eleven national championships and had produced quite a few NFL superstars such as Reggie Bush, Matt Leinart, Clay Matthews, Rey Maualuga, and Brian Cushing. USC *was* the gold standard and I wanted nothing less. When they offered me a full ride, my decision was easy. I knew I was meant to be a Trojan.

I hit the USC gridiron hard, with the goal of becoming extraordinary. Because I knew how quickly an NFL career could end—if mine even started at all—I hit the books just as hard as I would a tackling dummy or an opposing player. Education has always been very important to me, and I've always done well. It's not because I'm super smart, but because I worked hard and was dedicated to my studies. I knew that would give me some sort of an advantage later in my life. I didn't coast on USC's full ride, though. Instead, I took advantage of the free education that I had earned. I majored in communications, piled on extra courses, and graduated in three years. I continued for another year and a half and earned my master's degree in communication management and marketing.

My academic success was a worthwhile achievement, but note there had been no mention of it in my original game plan. Instead it was all about football, and the plan continued taking hits. What my game plan didn't account for were more football injuries in college. After my freshman year, I had thumb surgery. After my sophomore year, I had surgery to repair a grade 4 microfracture and a torn labrum in my hip. The doctors also shaved down my hip socket bone. Such an injury often ends athletic careers, so I consider myself fortunate that I was able once again to recover well enough from a major injury to play, although years later I still suffer from hip issues.

I was healthier for the start of my senior season at USC. The game plan was coming back together. I was fit and primed to have a great season, and eventually move on from school with my two degrees, when the unthinkable happened. During a weight-training session, my strength coach encouraged me to bench press 425 pounds for four reps, which was going to be a new max for me. The first two reps I got off my chest smoothly, but something went horribly wrong on the third rep, resulting in excruciating pain for me. The doctor's diagnosis: I had torn my pec muscle completely off the bone.

Sports media started its familiar doom-and-gloom approach to my situation, saying in so many words, "There's no way that Devon

Kennard is going to get into the NFL now." It dawned on me that they might be right.

It made sense. I had already sustained numerous injuries in the past five years, and it was a fair question to ask: How much more could my body take? Some in the media reported or opined that there was no way I would ever be able to play like a pro. I became discouraged; it was safe to say I was depressed, feeling down about life in general, because of what I was feeling as well as what I was hearing.

Because I was injured so early in the season, I was within my rights to take a medical redshirt year as a senior at USC. This meant delaying or suspending participation in football in order to save that fourth year of eligibility for the next year. During that time away from playing, I still worked my butt off to prepare myself to prove I belonged on the field again. It worked—*somewhat*. During my redshirt senior year, I made nine sacks and a total of fifteen tackles for losses, which were strong numbers. But I still couldn't shake being known as an "injury-prone guy." Media pundits projected me going, at best, in the sixth or seventh round of the 2014 NFL Draft—if I got drafted at all. I read that I would be "lucky" to be going as high as the sixth or seventh round.

I couldn't tune out what I was hearing, and I experienced a gnawing feeling that the media might be right.

What Life Do I Want?

Even though I was closer to getting into the NFL than ever before, I wondered: *What if I don't get drafted at all?* Up until now, my life seemed to be all rainbows and sunshine. I was the guy with the pro football dad. I had good grades and was the best athlete. I worked hard and it showed. It was the best start I could have gotten toward my dreams. And then injury after injury and surgery after surgery. I was bitter. I was upset. "God, why me!" I asked. But in the end all of this humbled me so much that I started thinking about what life looked like for me outside the game of football. I needed to find other outlets for happiness and other ways to be successful.

So I asked myself another question, one that would change the course of my life: *What life do I want?* Not what life my parents wanted for me and or what my coaches, teachers, or friends thought I should have. What type of life did *I* want? I had no doubt I wanted to be more than just Devon the football player.

One word popped into my mind. I wanted *freedom.*

I wanted the *financial* freedom to do whatever I wanted to do and have whatever I wanted to have while also being able to positively affect my family and also make a difference in the world (I'll talk about this more later).

As a young, Black male looking back, I know that I am one of the fortunate ones in that demographic. I have been the recipient of more opportunities than other Black males get. I have my mom and dad, Derek and Denise, to thank for that. They were born and raised in Stockton, California, which is well-known for being a dangerous city inundated with crime. They started dating in the seventh grade, and as young as they were, they were smart enough to know they would need to work especially hard just to make it out of Stockton and have a chance at building better lives for themselves.

My dad's football abilities earned him (and my mom) that ticket out of Stockton and into the pros, where he played for thirteen seasons, his time with the Dallas Cowboys culminating in a Super Bowl ring. I have always greatly admired my dad, not just for his playing in the NFL but more so because he—and my mom—worked hard to give my brother, sister, and me the kind of head start in this world that many minorities never get. Actually, as of 2021, the percentage of Black people living in poverty is 1.7 times greater than the US's total population, and they represent 22.6 of the poverty population.[2]

My dad told me to chase whatever dreams I had even if they weren't football. He wanted me to be happy at whatever I decided to do, and he never told me that I needed to do better financially than he did. He never pressured me in that regard. I figured it out on my own that it was my responsibility to take those blessings and advantages that my parents gave me and do even better for myself, my future family, and my children's kids. I wanted to flip the bag!

Dad and I didn't talk much about money, but he made sure to tell me about mistakes either he or his teammates had made. It boggled my mind that someone could play in the NFL, make so much money, and then end up broke just a few years after they retired. These guys didn't consider the fact that after their career was over, they would still have the likelihood of decades more living in front of them for which they would need money just to survive.

In his eye-opening *Broke* documentary for ESPN Films, director Billy Corben documented the lives of several professional athletes who earned millions in their respective sports only to lose most or all of it to drugs, lavish spending, bad investments, or bad advice. Some athletes get caught up in the fame and fortune of being in the pros, and they want to make it rain money wherever they go. There are players who don't understand the basics of personal finance and trust the wrong people to make decisions about their money.

That was *not* going to be me.

I promised myself that if I made it to the pros, I would save as much of my money as possible, learn as much as I could about saving and investing, and make the right decisions to protect my financial future. After all, if I play football until I'm thirty-five years old, I still have to support myself and my family not just for the rest of my own life, but even after I die, through life insurance and whatever kind of estate I leave behind for surviving family members. That could entail forty or more years of my having to provide a place to live, food to eat, clothes, health care, and so much more. So I needed to find other ways of making money (creating income streams) that would continue to support me even after my football career was over.

But before I could do that, I had to get drafted.

Making an Impression

It was time to turn it up and impress at the NFL Combine, a week-long camp where college draft prospects show NFL coaches what they're made of on and off the field. It's the ultimate "tryout" for football players. College prospects are on full display, walking around with nothing but tights on while league and team personnel measure every inch of our bodies and scan us for injuries. Prospects are also required to take a drug test and undergo an all-day interview. On the last day, they run a forty-yard dash against a stopwatch (your forty time, especially, then follows you everywhere you go in the scouting and then drafting process—lots of pressure for a fast time) and other agility drills to prove our athleticism.

On the field, I was doing well during the Combine, but off the field my health issues still shadowed me. And it wasn't just the history of injuries I already knew about. During my physical exam,

At the 2014 NFL Combine
Photo credit: Johnny Vy/NFL

medical tests uncovered an undiagnosed heart condition called dextro-transposition of the great arteries. That's the technical name for a serious but rare congenital heart defect in which the two main arteries are reversed. While consulting with additional cardiac professionals, I was told that this defect was something that I needed to monitor, but it would not affect my football career. *Thank God!*

New York Giants scouts closely watched me and three other players at the Combine and then flew the four of us to New York for interviews. The Giants' linebacker coach drew one of their defenses on a board and explained every player's job. Without advance warning, he then erased the whole thing and asked us to redraw what we had seen while we explained our position to him. That was unexpected and nerve-racking but a great test for us, and I wanted to go first.

During college I had been asked to play outside linebacker, defensive end, and even middle linebacker, all of which gave me a great understanding of defensive schemes and everyone's job. I was ready for this! Part of my game plan I had devised a year earlier. Not only was I able to draw and explain my position, but I drew and explained the entire defense and what each player needed to do during certain offensive plays. The coaches seemed really impressed, and the other prospects couldn't duplicate my success with the impromptu assignment. I left feeling confident.

Next Came the NFL Draft

I will *never* forget this date . . . the first day of the 2014 NFL Draft was May 8, 2014, almost three months after the 2014 NFL Combine. The NFL Draft has seven rounds and is spread over three days. Day one of the draft is just the first round; that is when you see the players who are drafted walk across the stage and hug Commissioner Roger Goodell. Day two is for the second and third rounds, and day three is reserved for rounds four through seven. The later you get drafted, the less money you sign for, the fewer guarantees you have in your contract, and the harder it is to make the team.

In my case, I knew that I was unlikely to get drafted on day one or two so I circled May 10, 2014, on my calendar. When the fourth round began, I watched other players whom I believed I was better than get drafted before me. I was extremely nervous and unstable, spending the morning in the backyard of my brother's house crying and praying to God that I would hear my name!

Please Lord, let somebody give me a chance.

By the grace of God my prayer was answered. During the fifth round, Giants head coach Tom Coughlin called to tell me that I had been selected to play for his team, as the 174th player taken in that 2014 draft. *Yes!*

Nobody can take that moment away from me. No matter what happened next, I had achieved my lifelong dream of becoming an NFL player. My game plan had worked.

The first thing I did after I got the good news was to go to a local mall to buy a New York Giants cap. That night, I went out to the club in Scottsdale and celebrated with my friends. I was having the time of my life, and here comes a woman walking toward our table with a mutual friend. *"Oh my gosh, who is that!"* I said it so loud that apparently everyone, including this woman, could hear me. I met Camille briefly that night, and this was the extent of our interaction. But a year later, life would bring us back together. She would ultimately become my wife and the mother to our children.

The next day, tired and slightly hung-over, I left for East Rutherford, New Jersey (where the New York Giants are based).

At the mall buying a Giants hat after I got drafted
Photo credit: Devon Kennard

Stay the course. If you give up when things get hard, you will never flip the bag. You may hit points in your life where things aren't going your way, but continue to trust His plan for your life and don't give up. Your dreams can be on the other side of your failure.

CHAPTER TWO

The Big Leagues

Be prepared to sacrifice what you are
for what you will become.

Here's a quick assignment for you. Go to YouTube and search "GQ Sports." Here you will find videos on NFL players such as Jalen Hurts, LeSean McCoy, Ronnie Stanley, and Justin Jefferson (to name a few) who break down exactly how they spent the first million dollars they received once they had made it to the NFL. For example, Ronnie Stanley, an offensive tackle for the Baltimore Ravens, bought a BMW X6 sports car ($120,000) and took a trip to Japan ($20,000).

Don't look at me. I barely spent any of my rookie signing bonus.

Believe it or not, I even had my 2005 Kia Sorento, which I had driven all through high school and college, shipped to me in New Jersey so I didn't have to buy a new car.

Let's look at the reality. I had signed a four-year contract with the Giants, but only a small percentage of that was guaranteed. I didn't even know if I was going to make the Giants final cut for that season or, if I did, how many years I would end up playing. Plus, I wasn't one of the big names in football like wide receiver

Odell Beckham Jr.—who was drafted by the Giants in the first round the same year I was—or Tom Brady, or any of the other players who already had big names in college. Granted, my last name might have had a ring of familiarity to mostly Cowboys fans because of my dad's having played there. Still, I had no idea if I would gain any fame, play more than a year, or make even a fraction of the money that some guys make. Nothing was certain, so I wanted to start my career by saving money and waiting until I knew for sure that I had a solid career before I bought anything substantial or luxurious. This is why I stayed frugal my rookie season.

Stayed frugal? Yes, that's correct. Growing up, my family called me stingy. That was a fair description. I never wanted to part with my cash. Friends and family knew not to ask to borrow money from me. I didn't spend a lot either. Sneakers—especially Jordans—were the only thing that I really enjoyed buying. Luckily my brother Derek and I wore the same size while I was in middle school and high school, so I would "borrow" his.

"Aren't you going to get a *real* car?" my new Giants teammates jabbed, but I didn't let their comments pressure me into buying something I really didn't want or need at that moment. Instead, I stayed focused on the financial goal I had. I could wait to buy a new car—delayed gratification is still gratification.

Buying or renting a lavish home as many guys did wasn't my thing either. Playing in New York, many players rented expensive high-rise apartments in either Hoboken or Edgewater, New Jersey. These are nice areas that overlook New York City and are close to MetLife Stadium, which the Giants now share with our AFC counterparts, the New York Jets. Not me. I rented a really nice but smaller and more affordable apartment. We were on the road a lot, so I didn't need anything big and pricey.

I was now making more money than I had ever seen up to that point in my life and had a lot to learn, but I didn't wait for someone to come along and teach me what to do. I dedicated each day to not only devouring the Giants playbook and learning about that week's opponent but educating myself about personal finance, reading whatever I could get my hands on, and listening to financial podcasts (I'll share my favorites later).

I finished my rookie season with a combined forty-three tackles (thirty-five of them solo), four and a half sacks, two forced fumbles, and a pass deflection—all accomplished in the twelve games (including six starts) in which I played. I experienced a few more health issues, including a pulled hamstring that cost me a few games, but overall it was a good first year for me.

DEVON DEBUNKS

The Secret Truth about Salaries in the NFL

 Let's talk about one of the most fascinating things about being an NFL player—the huge salaries. Don't let them fool you, because when you hear that your favorite player just signed a two-year, $10 million NFL contract, it's not telling you the whole story. In most cases, not all dollars talked about are guaranteed (like they are in Major League Baseball).

In actuality, that player's contract might have been written as a one-year contract with $6 million guaranteed and an *option* for year two. (An option means the team has the "option" to pay the rest of the contract or terminate it. They are not locked in to paying that money because it's not guaranteed.) In this example, the contract could look like this: a $4 million signing bonus and a

$2 million salary for year one, and a $4 million salary for year two that is *not* guaranteed. As long as they cut that player before the fifty-three-man roster is set at the end of training camp for his second year, the team will not have to pay that additional $4 million for year two. So that two-year, $10 million contract really only guarantees a one-year $6 million contract.

Uncle Sam then comes along and takes his share, which is a lot. An NFL player is in the highest tax bracket there is, getting taxed at around 37 percent, and that's just for federal *income* taxes! Depending on where a particular player plays and/or lives, he might be having to look at also paying a state income tax as well as whatever local taxes are, and both of those can vary from state to state (some states, such as Tennessee—where the Titans play— have no state income tax) and locale to locale. To give you guys insight on this, my Arizona tax rate—including federal and state— puts me at 44 percent, so let's use 44 percent in this example.

Next, let's use the example of a fictitious player to break this down. He has to pay his agent, who typically gets 3 percent of whatever the player makes before taxes. Now that we know that the $10 million, two-year contract actually is a one-year $6 million contract—with about 44 percent going to taxes and 3 percent to agent fees, that brings his guaranteed net down to around $3.2 million net. It doesn't stop there.

There are other expenses that an NFL player must pay, such as NFL Players Association dues, off-season training fees, and more, which will, of course, lower his take-home pay even further, to around $3 million or even less. So at least half his money is gone— or more than two-thirds if you count that original $10 million figure you saw in media reports—before he can start buying his fancy (or not-so-fancy) wheels or the lease to his glitzy (or not-so-glitzy) rental place.

Don't get me wrong—$3 million, give or take, is still a lot of money, but it's not $10 million or even $6 million. Fans think that an NFL player who is offered a $10 million contract means he gets a $10 million check to spend how he likes. Not exactly. Not even close.

Season Two: My First Side Hustle

Heading into my second season with the Giants (2015), a teammate asked me to go to a real estate seminar with him. That piqued my interest. While at USC, I had discovered the joy of learning about the real estate industry, so I said yes. It was at this seminar that we met an investor who made a bunch of money flipping homes on a large scale in Indianapolis.

The concept of flipping is simple. You buy a cheap home that needs renovating or has some type of value-added potential—aka a fixer-upper. Renovate it and resell it for a profit. This investor flipped hundreds of Indianapolis homes per year. He took us under his wing and taught us how. I wasn't handy and didn't have time to learn how to properly fix up homes, so flipping homes really wasn't for me. That's not the only factor that gave me pause about flipping. Flipping a home is a one-time transaction. Once you sell it, you won't generate another dollar in gain from that property. What happens is that you earn a lump-sum payment at the time of sale, but then you have to turn right around and stick that money into your next fixer-upper (buying it and then paying for labor and materials) and the whole process starts over again. Along the way you are, perhaps, putting a thin slice of those profits into your bank account. That's a lot to think about and deal with.

Even though many people make a good chunk of money using a fix-and-flip strategy, I would rather *own* that same property as a rental. I would lease it out to a tenant to generate consistent monthly cash flow while taking advantage of the appreciation of the property over time. Flipping homes wasn't the kind of opportunity that I was looking for at the time. I prefer investments that earn me money even when I'm sleeping.

Nevertheless, through this investor, my buddy and I bought a single-family house together. We each put $12,000 down on a three-bedroom, two-bath home that cost a modest $86,000 in Beech Grove, Indiana. It was a turnkey property, which means it didn't need any work and it even came with a tenant already living in it. We didn't flip it, we *owned* it.

My first investment property
Photo credit: Devon Kennard

Each month our tenant pays rent and we pay the mortgage and expenses, which includes a property manager to take care of and manage the home. After the expenses are paid, this property generated a few hundred dollars of profit each month. We started making money on day one.

You've Got Mailbox Money!

 Earning a few hundred dollars each month doesn't make us real estate moguls, but it started what is known as "mailbox money," or "passive income" for us. (For the rest of the book, I'll be calling it mailbox money because I prefer that term, but they are often used interchangeably.)

Mailbox money is the concept that you buy, make, or invest in something that provides you with consistent cash flow without really doing much more work (which is why it's also called *passive* income). It's mailbox money because, years ago, you would get cash flow in the form of checks in your mailbox. Now with direct deposit, it's mostly a figure of speech, but I still like to call it that.

The return (profit) we earned was about 8 percent annually, which is really good considering it was our first investment and the risk was low. I was excited to be bringing in mailbox money from something that wasn't football. Now you know why real estate quickly became something I would be extremely passionate about.

On the Field

After I had a hand in purchasing the Beech Grove property, I waited a little before I invested in another property, but this time it wasn't by choice. The Indianapolis flipper had a few big-time investors who bought all of his properties. That didn't include me, obviously, so he had no investment opportunities coming my way. That taught me a valuable lesson about how to pick markets where I could scale; owning and leasing out one property wasn't going to be enough to reach my financial goals at the time, which was $10K a month in mailbox money.

Until I figured that out, I focused my efforts back onto football. After all, I still had a lot of work to do with the Giants to make sure that my NFL salary continued for another year. I needed to keep the main thing (football) the main thing!

Stop me if you've heard this before: injuries continued to plague me in my second season with the Giants. I suffered from hamstring issues and a case of severe turf toe, both of which together held me back from playing a full season. I saw action in only nine of the Giants' sixteen regular-season games, but when I played, I had an interception and fifty-eight combined tackles. That year, Giants Blue went 6–10, finishing third in the NFC East division.

These injuries were harsh reminders that this game was tough on my body. Not only did I need to work hard at getting back on the field each time, but I also needed to work quickly to maximize my financial opportunities—just in case.

In 2016, I came back with a vengeance and had a great year, playing all sixteen regular-season games and combining for sixty-one tackles. Our coach, the legendary Tom Coughlin, resigned in January, and the team promoted offensive coordinator Ben McAdoo to take Tom's place. We went 11–5 in 2017, placing second in the NFC East, but we suffered a heartbreaking loss to the Green Bay Packers in a wild-card playoff game.

Getting a hit on Jameis Winston
Photo credit: National Football League

Financial Checkup: A Million-Dollar Milestone

Between seasons, I make it a habit to regularly check on my invest-ments. I started by traveling to Indiana to visit the Beech Grove property, where I was pleased to find out that everything was going well. I had also hit a financial milestone in my life at the start of 2017, accruing a net worth of $1 million. That's a lot of money for a twenty-five-year-old to have, and I wanted to be smart with it. I already thought about retirement, something that not many young people my age think about. I had fully vested myself in the NFL's 401(k) retirement account, which was my first real exposure to the stock market. In the locker room, there was always a group of guys talking about "making a killing" in the stock market, but those same guys were also kicking and screaming when the market was down. After giving it some thought, I decided to use some of that first million to invest in the stock market and see what it was all about. Through another teammate, I found an experienced financial adviser who was knowledgeable about how things worked on Wall Street. I worked with him, and we put together an investment strategy that fit my risk tolerance and needs.

In 2017, my fourth year with the New York Giants, my contract guaranteed a significant bonus, so now I was like, "Oh, let's roll!" The stock market was profitable, and I was doing okay, but I wasn't passionate about it the way I was about real estate. I was itching to get back into owning more.

Tip: Every time I hit a monthly
income goal, I increase it.

To make the real estate needle move in a way that would matter to me, I needed to invest in more properties. I was really hungry to start earning more mailbox money, but this time I decided to fly solo and not have a partner.

I hired my financial adviser whom I still work with today, who focused on alternative investments such as real estate syndications. He introduced me to a syndicator/investor who buys and flips properties in Cleveland, Ohio, and other markets throughout the US. Through this investor and using all cash, I bought six affordable turnkey properties in Cleveland, which quickly increased my monthly mailbox money significantly.

BiggerPockets

If you haven't been able to tell yet, I love to learn, so I read a lot and listen to a lot of podcasts. One of my favorites is *BiggerPockets: Create & Build Wealth with Real Estate Investing*, hosted by Brandon Turner and David Greene. In one episode, I learned about Nathan Brooks in Kansas City, where he flips homes and provides turnkey investments to investors like myself. I reached out to him in hopes of diversifying my portfolio. Through him, I bought six rental units in Kansas City, which increased my mailbox money yet again. (By the way, how I acquired the Cleveland and Kansas City properties is a great example of the power of networking, which we will talk about more in chapter 9.)

Special Access

Not only do I listen to the *BiggerPockets* podcast, but I also pay a yearly fee to access their online real estate calculators. These calculators make it easy to input information on properties I am considering buying to figure out if the numbers make sense. Often, people have issues with real estate investing because they do not understand how to underwrite deals on their own, create Excel sheets, and do the math. As a *BiggerPockets* pro member, I have unlimited access to courses, webinars, and forums. It's an easy way to get real-life teachings from current investors on a tried-and-true real estate website, https://www.biggerpockets .com. (FYI, they didn't pay me to endorse their site.)

Things were going really well for me back on the field for the 2017 season. In week 7, I had a season-high five combined tackles in one game against the Seattle Seahawks and a total of forty-one combined tackles (twenty-four solo), four sacks, and two pass deflections in fifteen games and eleven starts. I was inactive in week 10 because of a quad injury. However, the Giants didn't do well that season; we ended up going 3–13 and Ben McAdoo was fired.

The season ended as did my contract with the Giants, but because of how well I had played the previous four years, I believed I would be offered a new contract to sign. Unfortunately for me, the new head coach, Pat Shurmer, and general manager Dave Gettleman wanted to keep me but only if they could do it for a steep discount.

Here's a fun fact—I grew up *really* disliking the New York Giants. My father, Derek, won a Super Bowl with the Giants' biggest divisional rival, the Dallas Cowboys, so it was only natural for me to hate them. But after they drafted me and I moved to the East Coast, I fell in love with the culture and atmosphere of New York, and I really wanted to stay.

Unfortunately, the Giants offered me significantly less money than every other team that showed interest. I felt a bit disrespected because I knew I had played good ball. But let's just say that leaving the Giants was an eye-opening experience about the NFL business. I felt like I wasn't a valued player but instead a dispensable commodity.

But this also taught me that I needed to treat myself like a business. Even Jay-Z says, "I'm not a businessman. I'm a business, man!" That meant getting the best offer that I could possibly get, so I turned down the Giants offer and put myself in a much better position to accept a more lucrative offer from the Detroit Lions. It was time to flip the bag and multiply my blessings in a new city!

Fast-forward to 2022. A lot has happened between buying the Beech Grove property and now as I write this (summer of 2022). I'll share more of my journey later, but I played for the Lions for two seasons and am now with the Arizona Cardinals as we get ready for the 2022 season. With each move, my NFL salary grew significantly. I invested in even more rental properties and, as of January 2022, I owned nineteen units across several states. I created other ways to earn money as well. That included becoming a paid speaker, signing a contract for this book, and investing in syndicated real estate deals. As I'm about to show you, I followed what my passion was, which led to my NFL career. Now I am using my NFL salary to grow my investment portfolio, and my investment income will fund still more additional financial opportunities.

By sticking to my first game plan, I have flipped my first bag and started making my life look the way I wanted it to.

Looking back, I realized that I was following these five key steps to flipping the bag:

5 Keys to Flipping the Bag

1. Identify what you are good at and/or passionate about.
2. Become extraordinary at those things.
3. Use what you are good at or passionate about to maximize your earnings.
4. Use those earnings to create multiple income streams.
5. Repeat.

These keys give me direction and help me move down the field and closer to my financial goals. Once I'm done with one goal, I go back to the first key and start again. This time—real estate. Repeat. I follow these keys in all aspects of my life.

Today, I am:

- Devon the football player
- Devon the real estate investor
- Devon the public speaker
- Devon the author
- Devon the philanthropist

And each time I start a new journey, I follow my five step-by-step keys. You can do it, too.

Each key *you* complete gets you closer to your goals—it all adds up. In the NFL, every team has a playbook to help guide them to victory. Consider this book your own personalized playbook that will help get you to the life you've always dreamed of.

"But Devon, I don't make as much as a professional athlete."

Yes, I'm a pro football player who makes a large salary, but that was *my* dream. I'm sharing my journey to inspire you to create your own game plan and follow the keys I created to achieve *your* success. Whether you're a single mom or dad, an entrepreneur, fresh out of college, or near retirement, you can make changes in your life to achieve your own dreams and enjoy your own definition of financial freedom. Let's get to it!

Don't get bored with consistency. Find a process that works for you and stick with it. My five keys have worked for me over and over in my life, and I think they can do the same for you.

CHAPTER THREE

It's Your
American Dream

Your life doesn't get better by chance.
It gets better by change.
—Jim Rohn

Children in the Black community typically are taught that it isn't our place to ask our parents how much money they make, spend, or have in the bank. We are told that it is none of our business. When I was growing up, my family would have only casual conversations about money, or my dad would just say things like, "You got to be careful, son, or you can go broke." He and my mom wouldn't talk to us at all about their own finances.

It's ironic—even though talking to our parents about money is frowned upon in Black culture when we are kids, as an adult I have found it essential that we understand our parents' financial situation to help them have their affairs in order as they age. As their children, we want to help them and make sure they are taken care of, but how can we do that if we're not supposed to talk about their money earlier in life?

Over the years, I've observed the family dynamics of some of my friends of other races, and their conversations with parents seem much more open than what I grew up with. Parents and children in the Black community can learn from this.

Some lessons on finance I did pick up along the way are my dad's stories about how he and his teammates handled money over the years. Those things I heard stayed with me, so in a roundabout way he did teach me some dos and don'ts about how to handle finances. I never wanted to be as wasteful or careless with my money as some of my dad's teammates apparently were. I wanted to understand what money was all about and how to make it work for me. I wanted to make sure I made the right choices when it came to saving, spending, and investing. Most importantly, I wanted to make enough that I was living a life of financial freedom.

Financial freedom.

It had to be more, however, than to just state that I wanted financial freedom; I had to be the one who put the steps in place to *make* it happen. Every day, I get out of bed, work hard, and focus on doing *something that gets* me closer to the goals and lifestyle I knew that I truly wanted. I've been doing that for years now. The longer you do it, the more it becomes a part of a routine without drudgery. It's living a life of intent and living in the moment simultaneous to building for the future.

Breaking the Stereotype

There is a "dumb jock" stereotype that goes with being an athlete. I decided early on it was important for me to break through that. In the beginning I knew nothing about personal finance or real estate investing. So I resolved to educate myself. You can do that, too. I read a lot and talked to financial experts and real estate experts. During those opportunities, I asked many questions and absorbed as much information as they were willing to share with me. Then I made sure to take full advantage of every academic opportunity I had. My two degrees have opened doors for me to chase what I call *my version* of the American dream.

Generally speaking, the American dream is the idea that whether you are born in the US or immigrated here, you have the right to achieve prosperity and success no matter your social class or other circumstances. It *seems* like a great and fair concept when you hear it, but it's not relevant anymore. It's completely outdated and unachievable in many cases. That is why I call it "my version." Shocked? Don't be.

You might not realize that the reason you are struggling to achieve your financial goals is that you're chasing this practically unattainable version of the American dream. I have found that to be the case for many people I've met. Here's what the old model of the American dream looks like: You graduate high school, attend the four-year college of your choice, graduate, and get a nine-to-five job. Somewhere in there you meet someone special, fall in love, probably get married, buy your dream home and a fancy car, and raise a family. You go on to work for that company until you retire at age sixty-five, which is when you are given a gold watch as a thank-you as you walk out the door. Hopefully, when you're done with your years of company service, you retire with a nice nest egg because you have contributed to the organization's retirement plan, probably a 401(k). Don't forget Social Security benefits kick in around that time, too. Now you can ride into the sunset with enough money to (hopefully) enjoy your golden years. Congratulations, you achieved the American dream, supposedly accompanied by happiness, a sense of achievement, and financial freedom, already defined for you.

Sorry, but that's the flawed, outdated version of the American dream. If you're chasing this version today, you'll be left on the dock—that ship has long since sailed. What you might instead be looking at in the 2020s is massive debt, insufficient available funds to cover your golden years, and a nagging sense of unfulfillment. The dream has become a potential nightmare.

Why? Let's break it down:

Debt Degree

Studies show that more than half of all graduates leave college with their degrees and an average of $39,351 in student loan debt. Before you have landed your first job, you're weighed down by a heavy student loan debt load (and for many college graduates that debt anchor tied around their necks has reached six figures). School loan debt has become one of the biggest deterrents to reaching financial freedom. According to the Education Data Initiative,[1] one out of every ten Americans has defaulted on their student loans, and an average of 15 percent of student loans are in default at any given time. Is that what you want? I didn't think so.

Ask yourself: do you even need college? We are raised to believe that our path in life is supposed to consist of completing high school and moving straight onto a "good" four-year university; but that's not necessarily the path for everyone, nor should it be. Some students go to trade school or a two-year (community) college, or they go straight into the military or the degreeless workforce often described as "blue collar." I also know many young people who have gone to college out of obligation to their families or are just following the herd, because that's what they believe they are supposed to do. They go through life on autopilot.

Let's assume you *do* need college for your career. Would you want to end up with $35,000, $60,000, or more than $100,000 in student loan debt? Could you instead have chosen to attend a less-expensive college?

Some career paths absolutely need college degrees (and additional schooling in the case of attorneys, doctors, and so on). Be strategic, serious, and specific when deciding where you want to go to earn that degree. Let me make it a bit easier for you: don't choose the most expensive college or university because you think it's the best education you can get. Go where you receive the most funding in scholarship money or grants.

Alternatively, state or vocational schools and community colleges provide a perfectly good education with highly marketable degrees that can quickly lead to jobs and careers starting out with salaries higher than what many four-year schools' graduates are getting. You can get there with zero debt chasing you around for the next however many years. All you have to do is look around with an open mind. Be realistic.

Debilitating Debt

The average credit card debt in America stands at $6,270 per person.[2] If you have more month than you do money—with interest constantly being added to your remaining principal such that a huge chunk of whatever you earn goes toward paying off debt—how do you get ahead? So many people are so debilitated by credit card debt that they do not ever see a way out. That's even before we take into consideration your paycheck getting further carved up to pay Uncle Sam as well as to go for benefits such as health care.

Cars: Most people need a car, but buying one is the worst kind of investment; as soon as you leave the lot, it depreciates in value. Be intentional and mindful about the kind of car you buy and how much you are willing to spend, because a car is a bad debt that just costs money in the long run. If you can buy a decent used car—or what the sales folks now call preowned—perhaps buying it whole with cash—you are a big step ahead of the game.

Home: Then there's the symbol of the (old) American dream— homeownership. You dream of a three-bedroom, two-bath home with a backyard and white picket fence inside which kids can run around. You buy it—sometimes buying more than you can afford or really need—and are saddled with a mortgage for years. Unless you rent out a portion of it or tap into your home's equity (we'll talk about that later), you really do not make any money owning a home until you sell it. Buying a home to live in isn't a bad thing— for one thing, you can write off on your tax returns the annual interest you paid—but I get tired of people who keep saying you've made an awesome investment as soon as you bought it. For many people, it actually becomes the lit fuse to their financial demise. My advice: buy a home you can truly afford and can leverage in a way to get ahead financially.

If the bad debt is holding you back from achieving your goals, you're not alone. We are a society of consumers in which wanting more often means accumulating more debt, and beware financial counselors and bean counters who claim that debt accumulation is actually a good thing. What it is is a part of a vicious cycle.

Money Is the Big Divider

Last but not least is this part of the American dream definition I presented earlier: *regardless of their social class or other circumstances.*

It would be nice to believe that the same opportunities are available to all Americans regardless of social class or other circumstances that carry a bias, but we know that isn't true. The American dream is not a level playing field. To prove it, these statistics speak for themselves:

- In 2019, the average Black family had less than 15 percent of the wealth of the average White family.[3] The median wealth of White families was $188,200, compared with only $24,100 for Black families.
- Between January 1972 and December 2019,[4] other than during the aftermath of recessions, the African American unemployment rate stayed at or went above twice the White unemployment rate.
- In the second quarter of 2019,[5] the Black homeownership rate dropped to 40.6 percent, which is a 7 percent drop from ten years earlier. As of 2021, it was about 44 percent, while the White ownership rate was approximately 74 percent.
- When it comes to investing,[6] 71 percent of White Americans say they invest in stocks; only 55 percent of Black Americans do. When it comes to savings, Black Americans put away just $393 per month compared to their White counterparts' average of $693. That's according to the Ariel-Schwab Black Investor Survey.

- During the COVID-19 pandemic,[7] the unemployment
  rate for Black Americans has been 13.2 percent compared
  to 6.7 percent among White people, indicating a
  widening of the racial wealth gap.

It's time to bridge these gaps. Improving financial literacy and providing more financial opportunities for minorities will make a huge difference. Today's American dream is not only about making money and protecting your own financial future; it's also about educating and helping others do the same. Most importantly, it's *really* about giving everyone their fair chance at financial success.

When I played for the Detroit Lions, I worked with Midnight Golf, a nonprofit mentorship program based in Bingham Farms, Michigan. It helps walk metro-Detroit high school students through the process of applying for college and scholarships, taking SATs, and so on. Through Midnight Golf, I realized how many kids—especially minorities—have parents who didn't go to college. These kids are trying to change their own futures, but they don't know how to apply to college. Along those lines, they don't know how to research, find, and apply for scholarships and grants they desperately need in order to afford college. Midnight Golf helps to fill the gap for so many kids in the Detroit area. But this kind of help is needed in *every* city across America.

So if you're not earning enough income, have excessive debt, and have too many other obstacles in your way, replace worry with work. It's not too late to turn things around. Today, our lives are about more than working one nine-to-five job for decades only to earn a gold watch. Unless that's truly what you want your life to look like, in which case I'll show you how to leverage that nine-to-five income to create other income streams so you can further improve your financial position.

A Whole New World

The definition of the American dream mentioned previously has changed in recent decades. Some people even say there's a "new" American dream, although its interpretation depends on whom you listen to or read. While Americans want some of the same things their predecessors have sought—such as moving up the financial ladder to achieve prosperity and homeownership—they also want to start their own businesses and have their own definitions of work and freedom, as well as unprecedented flexibility with their time.

More and more people also want to toss the nine-to-five job aside. This desire is even more apparent with the success of Tim Ferris's book *The 4-Hour Workweek: Escape 9-5, Live Anywhere, and Join the New Rich*. This blockbuster hit the shelves and within five days was on the *New York Times'* bestsellers list. (This was after twenty-six out of twenty-seven publishers had turned down his book proposal; so how's that for determination!)

The new interpretation of the American dream is better than what it used to be, but it can be improved even further. I believe we should just throw out the "old" *and* the "new" versions. We are trying to take one concept and apply it to every American citizen and immigrant. Americans are not one-size-fits-all anymore, and the American dream shouldn't be either. Let's change that.

It's time to ignore every other version of the American dream and write your own version. Be a trailblazer in your own life. This will push you toward the way you truly want to live.

"My American dream is traveling the world while I write books."

"My American dream is being able to afford to stay at home with my children."

"My American dream is making enough money from playing music."

Your dream is going to look different from my dream as well as your best friend's dream. Good for you! The paths we take to get our dreams across the goal line are also going to be different. Today, there are more ways to make your dreams come true than ever before, and there is an abundance of information to help you learn how to do it—including this book, which is a great place to start.

But Devon, I don't even know what my version of the American dream is. I'm too busy working; I'm in debt, times are tough, and I just don't have time to even think about the future.

If you crave a change, make a change.

What life do you crave? Do not put any limitations on your answer. Do you want to quit your job and become a YouTuber? Or a professional gamer? Love your job and want to keep it, but just want to be debt-free? If your dream is to run your own business, don't worry if you don't have enough money or time to get started right now. Do not add negative commentary such as, "But I can't have that." Do not say, "My mother always thought that I should be . . ." No. What do *you* want your life to look like without obstacles in your way and without anyone telling you that you can't do something? Nobody is going to judge you.

Use this space to write down your answer:

_____

_____

_____

Acknowledging what you want is a great first step. Everything you do afterward should move you down the field toward that goal.

Find Your Passion

Still unsure what your American dream is? Start by working on the first key to success: find your passion. Ask yourself, *What am I good at or passionate about?* Better yet, what are you good at *and* passionate about? What are the things that make you smile and get you excited in the morning? Are you a singer? An artist? Good at designing tattoos? A football player? A budding entrepreneur? An inventor? Now, what are the things you are naturally really good at? Math? Coding? Video games?

Everything you are passionate about might not be what you're good at; likewise, everything you are good at may not be what you are passionate about. Think of ways you can combine what you are good at with what you are passionate about. Be creative.

You *can* have more than one passion, and what you're passionate about can change at different times in your life. Sports (specifically football and basketball) have been a passion of mine for as long as I can remember. I put a lot of effort into sports and became really good at them. When I was a junior in high school, I realized that I liked basketball just as much, if not more, than football. But I had to make a conscious decision to focus on football because I was better at football than hoops. My football skills made a game plan devised around football more sensible.

As I got older though, I found more things I was passionate about outside of football, such as real estate, public speaking, learning about financial literacy, networking, family, traveling, and philanthropy.

Write down a few things that you're either really good at or passionate about or both right *now*.

I'm good at and/or passionate about:

_____

_____

_____

Can you choose one around which to build your American dream, where you'll be happier and can make more money?

Let's say that you're passionate about cooking, but you work a nine-to-five job as a pharmaceutical salesperson for a *Fortune* 500 company. You're unhappy working for someone else, you're not making nearly enough money, you feel stuck. You can't quit your job because you need the money, but you're exhausted by the time you get home at night. Hard work is not the problem; working at a job about which you lack passion is the issue—it drains you. So you cook yourself a nice meal because that's your favorite part of your day. You then sit watching TV until it's time to go to bed. Rinse and repeat. Day after day, nothing changes, and you change nothing.

Time for a reboot.

Honestly, people find time for things that are important to them. So if cooking is what you're passionate about and that's the life you want, you need to find the time to start working on making this happen. Write down that it's your true passion.

Next, follow the five keys outlined in chapter 2 and start following them to help you achieve this dream. They say it takes thirty times of seeing or trying something new before it finally becomes a habit, so here are the keys again:

5 Keys to Flipping the Bag

1. Identify what you are good at and/or passionate about.
2. Become extraordinary at those things.
3. Use what you are good at or passionate about to maximize your earnings.
4. Use those earnings to create multiple income streams.
5. Repeat.

What would the keys look like for someone who likes to cook?

Become extraordinary: Each night you improve and enhance your skills until you're ready to cook for your friends and family.

Maximize your earning potential: You host cooking classes a few nights a week in your apartment or in someone else's home, or you offer a meal prep service for friends and family and advertise it on social media.

Create multiple income streams: You write and sell a cookbook of recipes that were handed down to you from your grandparents and great-grandparents. You offer cooking courses via YouTube. You create a meal prep website in the area you live where anyone can request meals.

With hard work, you gain enough students, cookbook sales, and customers to quit your day job and have the life you've always dreamed of. Or maybe you do not quit, but you have a business you manage on the side that brings you extra income and makes you much happier. But without taking that first step, none of this is going to happen.

And then *repeat.*

Hey Devon, what if I'm good at something, but not very passionate about it?

Connect what you're passionate about to something you're good at. For example, let's say you're *good* at Excel but you're not passionate about it. Maybe you're *passionate* about YouTube and you want to be a content creator. A great place to start would be to build a YouTube channel or online course where you teach others about Excel. You are using what you're passionate about— YouTube—*and* creating content to talk about something you're already good at.

At one time I wasn't super passionate about public speaking, but I identified it as something at which I'm naturally good. I always had good social skills and I am a good communicator. Talking is easy for me, but doing it in front of a crowd wasn't for me. That is until I realized that I can easily talk in front of any crowd about certain subjects—football, financial literacy, and real estate—all things about which I'm passionate. So I was able to combine public speaking with topics in my comfort zone. Now I use my public-speaking skills and real estate knowledge to bring in additional income.

If you know what you're passionate about and how you want your life to look, you're on the right track. But are you taking the next steps necessary to achieve it?

Let's say that you want to start a side hustle to make money to travel. Are you waiting for *something* to change? Nothing is going to happen by just waiting. You have to make it happen.

Are you devoting weekends to learning about this business you want to start? Did you write a business plan or research your idea? Have you looked into what it takes to run a business?

Start by investing in yourself. Buy a book on business or check some out of the library. Listen to podcasts. Take someone in your chosen field to lunch to pick their brain. Start learning business skills on YouTube, and so on. These are some free things you can do to improve your life as you get closer to opening your business.

Recall that Jim Rohn quote at the beginning of the chapter: "Your life doesn't get better by chance. It gets better by change." Even small steps are steps toward success, but you have to be the one to take that first step.

Breaking Perceptions

So what's stopping you from starting your business? Have you convinced yourself that there is no money available to start your business? Take time to research different funding opportunities. There are personal and business loans, Kickstarter campaigns, investors, and friends. All of these could be a good place to start when looking for funding. Besides, there are some successful businesses that have started out on shoestring budgets from proprietors' own savings accounts. Maybe a friend or family member—or a combination of several of them—would be willing to fund your start-up costs. All you have to do is ask, although it helps to have something to hand them, such as a business plan, or even a one-sheeter that outlines specifics and projections.

Finding the money to start your own business might be as easy as analyzing your own spending habits to free up some cash. Can you cut something out of your budget for a few months and put that money toward launching your business? Do you really need multiple streaming services? Cancel them and you might find a few hundred dollars are suddenly available. You can put that money toward supplies, marketing, or a website.

If you believe that you need to be debt-free or wealthy in order to own your own business or pursue an alternative revenue stream, think again.

Your success starts by changing your mentality about money and how it can work for you. Start by shooting that shot and speaking up because you never know where it will lead.

But Devon, what if I love my job and am already living out my passion? I'm just not making enough money.

You still need to think about your financial future. Does your job have a ceiling on earning potential? Will that ceiling be enough to provide for your family years from now? Only you can determine that. What if your family grows and you have more mouths to feed or put through school? What else do you want to do that you need to fund? If your income doesn't grow wherever you are working full time, you will need to build other streams of income.

Life Changes

When I was a kid, I was always asked by teachers or other adults a question commonly asked of kids, "What do you want to be when you grow up?" And we were expected to respond with one career, such as fireman, ballerina, doctor, football player—the list goes on. Nobody told us that we could have *more* than one aspiration, and most importantly, nobody taught us that our career, dreams, and goals might change at different phases of our lives and that it would be okay if and when that happened.

For example, maybe you wanted to be a teacher. You worked hard, earned your teaching degree and license, and molded young minds for years. Then somewhere along the way you discovered new passions. You discovered that you were a good artist and wanted to have your paintings hanging in a museum. When that happens, you don't have to leave your teaching profession, not if you love it. You can build a side hustle selling your work through art shows. You can also ramp up your side hustle enough to leave your teaching job if that's what you want.

Let's say you became your kids' soccer coach. You love it so much that you want to become a full-time soccer coach, maybe for a high school or university. It's not impossible. If you work hard at it, stick with it, and make some good contacts, you can make it *probable*. Life is not stagnant; neither should your dreams be. The vision you have for your life now will likely change and evolve over time. Again, I just wish my generation, when we were really young, had been taught that this is how things happen. Maybe we wouldn't struggle so much with change if we knew.

I have a close friend who is a reporter and is married with three kids. The reporter's lifestyle—long hours and travel—does not allow her much time to spend at home with her family. So she started a side hustle selling shampoo through Monat for extra income. After a year and a half of selling shampoo on the side, her revenue increased enough that she was financially able to quit her reporting job and become a full-time Monat entrepreneur. Now she makes her own work schedule and can spend as much time with her family as she wants.

Life also changes because industries change. Your position— even if you love your job—at some point may no longer be deemed necessary, and you are out of a job through no fault or flaw of your own. Your company might even go out of business. You might no longer be able to physically do the job that you're doing now, or maybe your company just fires you and decides to go in a different direction. You might enjoy your job now, but maybe you're not earning enough to support your family, so it's time to think about a new dream.

Life is not about one long, straight path to your goals. It's about paving your *own* path to your goals and adjusting it along the way. The era of getting a job and sticking with one company for an entire working career appears headed to extinction. All day, any day, if you listen or read enough, you'll keep hearing new stories about people who chase different dreams and live unconventional lives, all in the name of financial freedom.

Even with all the changes in the workplace and with careers— some of that certainly influenced by the recent COVID-19 pandemic—one important thing really needs to be changed, and that is the lack of financial literacy among citizens. The good news there is that you can immediately start doing what you can to educate yourself about personal finance. There have never been so many resources readily available for you to use.

I've already figured out the five steps for you, so now we're going to take that map and start moving down the field.

Keep in mind these wise words of the late South African theologian Desmond Tutu: "There is only one way to eat an elephant: a bite at a time." You won't accomplish these five keys overnight, but every actionable step (or bite) you take will help that goal become a reality. What are you waiting for? The first steps you take today will help you to drastically change your life tomorrow in a direction that you'll absolutely love.

Don't overestimate the competition
and underestimate yourself.
You are better than you think.

—Tim Ferriss

 We are all unique individuals with many different desires, talents, and skill sets. Identify what life you want for yourself, because we live in a society where it's easy to follow the herd. Recognizing what you are naturally good at and/or passionate about is a great place to start. Be a trailblazer!

CHAPTER FOUR

Maximize Your Earnings

No one cares more about your money than you!

"Hey, son, every time you get a sack this year, I'll give you a hundred dollars," my father told me the summer before my sophomore year in high school. I thought it was a brilliant idea. LOL.

That year, I put up seven sacks and earned $700. In my junior year, my dad decided to do it again. I started week 1 with five and a half sacks and by the end of the season, I had set both the Arizona high school and national high school sack records with twenty-four and a half sacks. *Cha-ching!* I made $2,450! Did I ball harder because I knew there was a hundred-dollar bill waiting for me after each sack? Of course I did. So I asked my father about paying me for sacks for my senior season.

"Oh, no," he laughed. "We're *never* doing that again."

Ha! I couldn't blame Pops for holding on to his wallet this time, but I did learn a valuable lesson about how hard work could pay off financially for me.

What I *didn't* know back then was what to do once I had the money in my hands. I knew nothing about money management other than how to earn it, spend it (of course), and *maybe* put at least some of it in the bank. Other than buying a pair of Jordans and a nice dinner at Olive Garden, I don't remember where the rest of that $2,450 went.

Even though the "flipping the bag" parable intrigued and inspired me to want to do the same for myself financially, I didn't actually know how to go about it. Do I just keep my money in the bank and it magically grows? Do I invest it? Do I do both? Do I do something else?

Interestingly, there is so much debt in America, yet not nearly enough education available about money, either in the home or in our public schools. From the time we are young, we should be taught how to earn, save, and invest. Everyone should be required to take personal finance classes in school so that once they graduate they will have a solid financial education and can make decisions about their financial future.

In college, my prerequisite classes were on the evolution of monkeys and astronomy. *Why?* Shouldn't prerequisite college courses include basic skills that we need in our lives, regardless of career path? I vote to start with subjects such as personal finance, investing, and basic accounting. Had I been taught any of this stuff earlier in my life, it would have made a huge difference when I was holding that rookie signing bonus in my hands after I was drafted.

To be fair, some universities do offer courses on financial literacy and personal finance, but most of them are tied to degrees that require such knowledge, such as business or finance. Every college student should be exposed to these courses, not just business and finance majors.

Interestingly, society was great at teaching me how to *spend* my money. Like many other Black teens, I looked up to entertainers who made millions only to spend it on frivolous, material things. Maybe they did it because, in comparison, Black people didn't make that kind of money, so as soon as we get some, we want to show it off and differentiate ourselves—like, "Ya man, I'm that dude! I made it!" Success became synonymous with spending.

Even in today's NBA and NFL, a player's "fits" (short for outfits) get them in front of the camera, so some players buy very expensive luxury fits to look good in pictures. I know some dudes who never wear the same clothes twice!

It wasn't until I got older and started meeting other wealthy individuals that I realized that there is more power in being a person who *can* buy anything he wants but chooses *not* to. (Just so you know, I'm not saying that once you become successful you can't buy nice clothes or frivolous material things, but this is all about making mindful decisions and asking yourself the reason behind every purchase.)

When you were a kid and got money for your birthday or Christmas, did it burn a hole in your pocket wanting to be spent? You probably begged your parents to take you to the store as soon as possible so you could spend it. I doubt that you begged your parents to put all or even some of your newly acquired savings in an actual savings account or buy stocks with it.

Today's teenagers are encouraged to spend money on video games, electronics, the coolest clothes, the latest shoes, and whatever else is trendy at the time. Why aren't they taught that there are other things they can and *should* do with their money? Imagine if you were taught how to invest some of it so it would work for you instead of you just working for it. Do you wonder how different your financial life would be today if you got a great start to your financial education?

For example, let's talk about the multiple pairs of Nike sneakers that line the bottom of many people's closets. If you love Nike so much, why don't you own *at least one* share of Nike stock? If you had invested just a little bit of the money you used to buy sneakers into the company, you would probably have already made that money spent several times over. That way, Nike would essentially be paying *you* to wear their brand, and you would still have a closet filled with your favorite sneakers. (Of course, there are risks in investing in the stock market, and you should talk to a professional and do your own research before making any investments).

Let me be clear about this: you can still enjoy life and do or buy the things you want, but do it wisely. Choose one to two things you like to spend your money on and cut back on everything else. I love traveling and eating out, but I cut back on fashion, cars, jewelry, and other things. People who struggle the most financially have too many vices. If you spend a bunch of money on all of them, you can't expect to get ahead.

We've also been taught to spend our money on the home we live in because we're told it's a good investment, the interest paid each year is tax deductible, and, after all, a man's (or woman's) home is his/her castle, right? It's also usually our life's first major asset (for many Americans it's their only asset) and part of that old-fashioned American dream. Owning a home in itself is fine. I own one. It was something I had dreamed of for a long time. But the home I now live in was not the first home that I bought. Buying a home to live in is an investment, but let's not ignore the fact that in most cases, while you are living in the home it is *costing* you money not *making* you money. I consider an asset as anything that generates revenue for me or appreciates, while a liability is something that costs me money. Therefore the home I live in is an asset that carries many characteristics of a liability. I think this is important for people to acknowledge and consider. (I'll dive deeper into this later in the book.)

You might have tunnel vision about money because your knowledge is limited. You like Nike, so you buy their shoes and not their stock. You want to own a home, so you buy a single-family house and never even consider buying an investment property. There's a better way to do this and everyone should be taught how.

What's Your $$ Personality?

Everyone has a money personality: it determines how you manage or relate to your finances. Maybe you are a saver, a spender, a moneymaker, a worrier, or a gambler. Determining which of these you are—or perhaps another type not mentioned here—can help you reel in your financial habits and make them work for you.

For example, Nicole was unable to figure out why she couldn't get ahead on her finances. She was making a good salary but always felt like she was behind where she *thought* she should be for someone almost thirty years old. It was when she took an online money personality quiz that she gained valuable insight into her money habits. Her mother, a single mom, was always worried about money and paying bills. It's no wonder that Nicole's money personality was that of a worrier. But once she reviewed her finances with a professional, she realized she was on a path to do pretty well. She just needed to change her mindset.

Find an online quiz that gives you a true idea of your money personality. Myers-Briggs and Marcus by Goldman Sachs created a free one that I would recommend.[1] (Be careful because you shouldn't have to pay for your results. Some financial institutions ask you to sign up for their newsletter or information, but you should never feel pressured to spend to get this information.) Let this start a conversation to get your finances in shape and provide you with a path for the future.

Studies show that most parents are pretty uneasy about teaching their kids about money. It might be because they don't know much about personal finance themselves. It's hard to teach your children how to save and invest money, especially if you are embarrassed about your own finances, are barely surviving paycheck to paycheck, and just can't save any money. On the other hand, if you don't have money conversations with your kids, you risk setting them up to do exactly what they saw you doing with your money—good *and* bad. Then the cycle continues until someone in the family's generational lineage finally breaks it. So *you* be the one to break it. With the right mindset and knowledge, we all have the ability and, hopefully, the opportunity to change our financial futures, even *if* our own parents struggled and failed to teach us what we needed to know. As of right now, the buck stops with *me* and *you*.

So where do you start?

I freely admit that I'm rarely the smartest person in the room. (I actually prefer it that way because I love seeking out someone who is smarter than me, and therefore I can learn from them.) Ever since I realized that I was on my own to learn about money, I have taught myself enough to help me achieve my financial goals and then some. How? I put the work in. I read, ask questions, listen, and learn—*and I never stop*. I share in this book what I learned along the way, my desire being to give you a basic financial insight and perspective that can steer you in the right direction. Then it is up to you to keep educating yourself. Become an owner and investor and not just a consumer and spender. I promise you that spending the time learning everything you can will keep you moving down the field just like it did for me.

It all adds up.

DEVON DEBUNKS

Cash Flow Is King

 When I'm asked what the most fundamental piece of money advice I can give is, I say, "Cash *flow* is king." That's different from "Cash is king."

It's your *cash flow*, not just your *cash*, that unlocks opportunities. Let's say that you have $100,000 in the bank. That's a lot of *cash*. If you do nothing else with that $100,000, it will earn minimal interest, meaning it won't cover you forever if you have to tap into it to cover expenses or pay for things you want. You still need cash *flow*, which is why it's king.

Now, if you're bringing in a cash flow of, say, $5,000 a month in mailbox money on top of the money you have earned and saved from your day job, you have more opportunities to do what you want and get what you need. Or you can just use that money to reinvest and grow it into even more. Both strategies are winners. I would rather have $100,000 in an investment versus cash in the bank because the investment is consistently giving me mailbox money, especially in 2022, when interest rates on mortgages reached greater than 6 percent.

Real estate entrepreneur Grant Cardone puts it this way: "Cash is trash." That means as soon as he has extra cash in the bank, he puts it toward another asset that can give him even more cash flow. Cash flow begets more cash flow, one on top of the other, and that's a good thing.

Your Life . . . Insurance, Trust, and Will

I am going to take a brief detour here to jump over to several topics that have a connection to money management and future planning—I'm talking about wills, trusts, and life insurance. They are tremendously important for protecting the financial future of your family should something happen to you. Nobody enjoys thinking about it, but before you take one more step forward, make sure you're doing what you can to protect your family if and when they have to go on without you.

Will and Trust: Do you have money? Do you own property? Do you have investments? If the answer to any of this is yes, be aware that without a will and trust, everything you own could go to arbitration upon your death. That essentially means your family might have to go to court and fight for the right to all of your assets. That's the last thing any family should have to go through after the death of a loved one. In a will and trust, everything is spelled out exactly—who gets what, including who becomes the guardian of your children. Writing a will is a relatively inexpensive thing to do, but it makes dealing with your death easier for your family.

Nothing is worse than a sudden death with no documentation in place. Setting up a will and trust is powerful; it shows that you have taken the time to consider your family and outline your wishes.

Life Insurance: Life insurance is about more than just paying for your burial expenses. I am a father of two beautiful girls, and I can't imagine how hard life would be if something happened to me and Camille was left to raise them on her own. Camille is paving her own way in the real estate industry and bringing in her own salary and mailbox money, but when someone passes on it adds a lot of stress to the family dynamic. A death benefit allows her to have a financial cushion and focus on herself and the kids without having to worry about money.

It's important to note that having life insurance is a must, no matter how much money you make. In the Black community, life insurance has been a complex subject. Studies have shown that Black Americans typically have only one-third the coverage their White counterparts possess, according to a 2020 study by insurance company Haven Life.

While both groups of Americans, on average, had less than the recommended amount of life insurance, Black Americans carried life insurance equal to only a year's income while Whites had almost three years' worth of such coverage. Once COVID hit, the 2021 Insurance Barometer Study revealed that the majority of Black Americans who own life insurance went up to 56 percent, which was three percentage points higher than 2020 and four points higher than the general population. That's an improvement, but those numbers simply aren't high enough. Truthfully, *all* Americans aren't taught enough about the importance of life insurance.

There are several types of life insurance—term, whole, universal, and variable—and it's important to talk to a fiduciary financial adviser about which type is right for you and your family's needs. Term is the least expensive type of life insurance, which is good if you're not making a lot of money. You want some protection for your family. I carry both whole life and universal life policies for my wife and me.

Stop Expense Creeping

By the way, while you're learning about money basics and how to maximize your earnings and get out of debt, don't get too aggressive in cutting your expenses. I call that *expense creeping*, which translates to your not looking at the bigger picture. The bigger picture should show you growing your income and earning potential, not just focus on cutting your expenses. Yes, cutting out cable TV or your favorite daily latte will save you money (and probably make you grumpy), but starting a business (even one on the side), learning or mastering a career or skill that pertains to your current job, investing in real estate or stocks, and so on will earn you much more over time. Put the majority of your energy into developing skills and tasks that generate much more revenue than what a latte costs. Then, use that revenue to pay off your debts even faster and start saving.

Just know that once you can get out of debt,
nobody can hold you down anymore.

If you're drowning in debt, it's difficult to think about saving money, but you will need money for emergencies and surprises as well as for investing and growing that income stream. Try to save something out of every paycheck, gift, job bonus, or tax refund you are given—*it all adds up.*

 Your physical, mental, and emotional well-being are extremely important, but it's time we add your financial well-being into the same conversation. Make it a priority in your life just like the others. Be mindful of this because each affects the other three.

CHAPTER FIVE

It *All* Adds Up

Give a man a fish, he can eat for a day.
Teach a man to fish, he can eat for a lifetime.

Darren Hardy wrote *The Compound Effect*, a bestselling book in which he explains how huge rewards are generated by small, seemingly insignificant actions. I firmly believe in this concept, especially when it comes to building wealth. That comes by intentionally practicing healthy *financial* habits on a daily basis the same way you take care of your physical, mental, and spiritual health. You are rewarded every time you learn something new. Every strategy and change you implement moves the needle closer to a bigger bank account and a life you've always dreamed of.

This is why improving your financial literacy is the first—and probably the most—important step to achieving the life you want. What you learn and how fast you learn it will determine how long it takes to get to where you want to go. Once you start making money, you need to know what you will do with it other than sticking it in a checking or savings account and letting it baste. Without the right financial know-how, your money will be gone in a heartbeat. Then you'll be back to square one. Now is the time to create positive financial habits. It might be tough, but the payoff will be huge.

(Spoiler alert: Learning never ends. You will always be learning something new about your money as you get older.)

But Devon, my financial situation is hopeless.

Change how you think about your situation. In a podcast interview, Emmy and Grammy Award–winning actress and comedian Tiffany Haddish opened up about her early struggles in the foster care system. Once she aged out, she was homeless and living in her car while trying to break into the entertainment industry. It was fellow comedian Kevin Hart who helped her turn things around. He gave her a few hundred dollars and told her to get a place to stay for a week. Hart suggested the following to her: "Put your goals out in front of you so you know what they are." She cried when she talked about how she didn't have parents to teach her about money, but that didn't stop her from learning on her own. Today, she is a multimillionaire and is working on giving back by opening up grocery stores in communities where they were lacking. She is also working on improving financial literacy so that no child has to go through what she went through, with no one to guide her.

It's *never* too late to turn your circumstances around.

But Devon, I'm too busy.

Maybe you are busy working, caring for the kids or aging parents, but if you can tell me what's going on with the latest episode of *The Bachelor*, something needs to change. If you're sitting on the couch watching every MLB game or playing hours of *Call of Duty* with your friends, something needs to change. If you don't know the difference between a will and a trust or what the different life insurance options are, something needs to change. If you're living paycheck to paycheck and in a boatload of debt, *you must find the time to change something,* anything! Don't complain that your life isn't going the way you want it to go if you're not actually doing something about it. You can find the time to work on improving your financial health, but not if you're spending every second of it doing something else. Financial literacy must be a priority no matter how busy you are.

Make it a priority to learn and grow so you have a positive relationship with money—even if you just learn a little at a time. Get up early and read books and magazines. Or listen to podcasts on a commute to work, while you're jogging, or at night after the kids go to bed. Take free online courses or check with your local library for free financial programs they might offer.

But Devon, I will hire someone to handle this for me.

You need financial professionals on your team at some point— an accountant, certified financial planner, and attorney for starters. But like I said, "Nobody's going to care about your money more than you!" I learned this lesson the hard way, which is why I never forgot it.

Once I started my third season with the New York Giants, I began investing in syndicated real estate deals. Simply speaking (I get into more detail in chapter 12), syndications are partnerships with investors who combine their skills, resources, and capital to purchase all kinds of real estate (for example, residential, commercial, industrial, storage, hotels).

I thoroughly enjoy investing in syndications. As I write this, I am in more than thirty syndications. At one point, however, I had so much on my plate that I wasn't paying attention to the numbers. I also bought more investment properties and had multiple stocks that I needed to keep an eye on, not to mention my football career. Turns out I was taking on too much.

Although thankful to be making more money, I got so wrapped up in everything that I started straying away from my own financial habits. I had hired financial advisers just as I should have, but I depended on them and trusted them way too much. I wasn't following up and occasionally eyeballing my numbers to see what was going on with *my* money. Big mistake! At one point, I couldn't even name the investments I was in or tell you how they were performing. When I finally did look, two of them had been severely underperforming for almost six months. I hadn't even noticed! At that point, I realized I had to rein in what I was doing and take back control.

From that point on, I made sure I fully understood every investment I was part of. I told my team to provide me with quarterly updates on my entire portfolio. Don't give anyone else more knowledge and control of your money than you would have if doing it alone. Imagine how much money I would have lost if I had continued to be so negligent.

Stay on top of where your money is going, no matter how much money you have.

Learn by Watching

There are many YouTube videos and television shows you can watch to learn about personal finance. One of my favorites is *Mad Money with Jim Cramer*. You also can learn a lot by watching the people around you. Just by walking around the players' parking lot, I learned how my Giants teammates were spending their money. There were all sorts of lavish cars, including Rolls-Royces.

Then I noticed what Eli Manning was driving.

Manning, the Giants starting quarterback and the team's highest-paid player at that time, drove to the stadium in a Toyota SUV. It's important to note that Manning's salary at the time was $15.1 million, yet he was driving to work in a car that cost him somewhere between $35,000 and $50,000 (depending on how much he had it tricked out), but I found out that he had leveraged his position with the Giants to sign a partnership deal with Toyota in 2004. He was actually being paid to drive his car! I made a mental note of that as I closed the door to my old Kia and drove away.

When Eli was asked in a 2013 interview if he really did drive a Toyota or if he had a secret Rolls-Royce at home that the public didn't see, he responded, "No . . . no . . . no! Ha ha. I drive a Toyota Sequoia every day, and it works out well. My backseat is folded down; the third row, too. I've got it loaded up with cleats and footballs, cones and, you know, during the spring it's golf clubs. It's loaded up with everything I need to do my job . . . it's more like a storage unit back there, but it keeps my life in order."

Look around. Do your neighbors own the latest tech gadgets and the best cars, yet you hear them always saying how money is tight? How is that possible? Are they just trying to keep up with the Joneses, but they really can't afford to? You might envy what they own, but you can learn a valuable lesson about how not to spend your money by watching how others are doing it, too.

Learn by Reading

Books have had a tremendous impact on me. One of the best personal finance books I ever read was *Rich Dad Poor Dad,* by Robert Kiyosaki. I learned a lot from his portrayal of two "dads"—one who accumulated wealth because of savvy investing, while the other—believed to be Kiyosaki's own father—worked hard but never was able to enjoy financial independence. It was an eye-opening introduction to personal finance for me.

With my favorite books
Photo credit: Devon Kennard

Another fantastic read is Tony Robbins's *Money: Master the Game: 7 Simple Steps to Financial Freedom.* But some books that have impacted me are not personal finance books. I enjoy reading autobiographies of successful entrepreneurs, athletes, and entertainers, and I've learned so much about life and business from them.

For example, hip-hop icon Rick Ross has written multiple books. In his *The Perfect Day to Boss Up*, he called himself a serial entrepreneur with a diversified portfolio. He is a multiplatinum-selling, Grammy-nominated recording artist who has leveraged his success into becoming the founder of Maybach Music Group. Plus he owns fast-food restaurant franchises as well as wine and spirits businesses, and he has started his own line of potato chips and ramen noodles. He created a line of hair care and men's grooming products. Rick is a partner in a sports agency, rents out his home to film studios for major motion pictures, and owns a cannabis company. He invested in companies that will provide him with mailbox money for years. Boy, I learned a lot from him.

Then there's the aforementioned Kevin Hart, who had his own challenging start in showbiz. In his books, including *I Can't Make This Up: Life Lessons*, Hart talks about how he took a bus from Philadelphia to New York City to perform, sometimes getting paid only in food. Today he's leveraged his success into forming his production company, the Laugh Out Loud comedy network, bestselling books, a men's activewear line, and so much more.

In *Shoe Dog: A Memoir by the Creator of Nike*, I learned that Phil Knight started his sneaker empire with only five hundred dollars! He wrote, "So that morning in 1962, I told myself: Let everyone else call your idea crazy . . . just keep going. Don't stop. Don't even think about stopping until you get there, and don't give much thought to where 'there' is. Whatever comes, just don't stop."

So if those successful entrepreneurs can take their passions and gifts and what little money they had when they started and leverage it all into a life they always wanted, I know that I can do the same. So can you.

Book Club

When I was with the Giants, I started #ReadingwithDK, a community to inspire future leaders to read. My wish for them was to discover there is a lot to be gained from reading and to just realize that reading is pretty cool. I pick a book for my followers to read, post it on my Instagram account, and then we talk about it and I give out prizes. Feel free to follow me on Instagram and all other social media sites @DevonKennard and join in on the fun!

Learn by Listening to Others

It's important to connect with those who have walked the path you want to take. These experts—whether financial or whatever field interests you—are filled with knowledge and experience and are often willing to share it (just be careful what advice you take until you have enough knowledge to determine the right decision for you). Listen.

When I was in college, I learned the importance of networking and listening to those who knew more than I did. Mike was the first mentor that I met while I was at a USC event. He had played for the Trojans, then went on to play for four years in the NFL with the Buffalo Bills and the San Francisco 49ers. I was drawn to him. He had a confident aura that people gravitated to.

As soon as Mike told me he was in real estate, I leaned in, eager to hear what he had to say and how he had made the transition from the NFL to commercial real estate development. He has since closed more than $1 *billion* in transactions.

Mike gave me his business card and I followed up a few weeks later. I asked him if we could meet to talk about real estate, and he said yes. Once we got together, I hung on to every word he said. I didn't really know much about commercial real estate. He opened my eyes to a whole new world by taking me to various buildings he was selling. Along the way he explained the commercial real estate business and how much the properties were worth.

I also met Stuart, another mentor who created wealth by purchasing golf courses. He even invited me out to one of his venues to swing the sticks, even though I have absolutely no idea how to play golf! Let's just say I was tearing up the course and not in a good way. He did give me one unforgettable golf tip, which was that a lot of business is conducted on the golf course. I listened as he taught me the value of ownership and hiring people so you don't have to do all the work. Back then, it affirmed that I wanted to one day own my own businesses and real estate properties just like him.

I then met Kyle, another USC alumnus who had played basketball and, it turns out, had the most direct impact on my desire to invest in real estate. Kyle did not become a professional athlete. He was a teacher who later became a police officer in Los Angeles County. He also became the cofounder and managing member of a large real estate investment and property management company in Los Angeles.

I listened as Kyle talked about how he and his wife became successful in real estate on a modest teacher and police officer's combined salary. They started by buying one small property and then slowly stacking up their purchases. Kyle and his partners now own more than fifteen hundred units and manage more than seventy-five hundred with a total of $2.75 billion in assets under management in the greater Los Angeles area. By listening, I learned that becoming successful in real estate was doable no matter what your salary is. He was the reason I knew that real estate was key to unlocking *my* American dream.

By the way, remember what I said in the last chapter—becoming financially independent doesn't mean you have to quit one job to do something else that is more lucrative. It's about finding what you're passionate about and leveraging that in a way that *becomes* lucrative. In Kyle's case, he had become extremely familiar with the areas he was patrolling as a police officer. In so doing he learned which ones were better to invest in and then leveraged that knowledge into wise investments. Kyle couldn't change his policeman's salary, but it's inspiring to know that he could use what he learned to benefit his side hustle. I credit Kyle with opening my eyes and giving me a vision of what I wanted my life to look like, with or without football.

Listening *is* learning.

Shoot Your Shot!

It's time! You've spent some time reading this book and maybe other finance books and magazine articles. You've watched hours of YouTube videos and maybe invested in yourself by taking a course about money. What can sometimes happen now, though, is that you can get stuck in the learning phase but not yet act on it— maybe you just enjoy the reading aspect of it, with one book generating a taste for the next one you now want to read. Digesting as much information as you can about investing, personal finance, or entrepreneurship is great, but at some point you have to come out from behind the information and take your first shot.

For example, if you are learning about real estate investing, you should eventually purchase a piece of property, even a small one. If you're learning about entrepreneurship, take that first step in starting your own business—whether it's applying for a license or ordering supplies you need to make your product.

Yes, you *will* make mistakes and learn lessons that you wouldn't have learned if you stood on the sidelines, but you'll fix them and build confidence along the way. The lessons I learned and the confidence I built from shooting my shot on my first real estate deal snowballed into the portfolio I have today.

If you want financial independence, the barrier to entry is financial literacy, so take the time to learn about finances and make it a priority in your life! You can only do this by building habits into your life that makes it automatic. Decide on something you can do daily, weekly, and monthly that will help you improve your financial literacy.

CHAPTER SIX

Maximize Your Mindset

Talent is a gift. Greatness is a choice and a mindset.
—Tim Tebow

I was a big kid (especially in terms of weight), so in order for me to play youth football I needed to get down to a certain weight. That meant I had to diet and drop the extra pounds I was carrying. I *begged* my parents to let me play, and they said yes. So for months I ate *soooo* many salads with chicken and hard-boiled eggs flavored with only oil and vinegar that I lost count. (To this day, I still hate hard-boiled eggs on my salad!) But it was my first taste—so to speak—of setting a goal and then maintaining a positive mindset to achieve it.

My mom didn't want me to diet like that again, so the next year I joined a league across town with kids older than me but more my size. I enjoyed playing in this league. It forced me to grow up quickly, and I gained a lot of confidence on the field. I realized that if I could do well playing football with the older kids, then I could dominate in my own age group, and that would be a big advantage to my playing development.

To this day, I can't stand hardboiled eggs on my salad.
Photo credit: Egidijus Bielskis on Unsplash

I have since done my best to maximize a positive mindset on and off the field.

That was put to the test when I got to high school. My brother, Derek Jr., had decided not to pursue an NFL career and instead chose to obtain his certification as a professional trainer. He then opened Pro Edge Performance Training in Chandler, Arizona, and became my personal trainer and coach. My brother is almost ten years older than I am, which helps explain why he was another father figure to me while we were growing up. I knew that nobody else could be better than him in getting the best out of me.

You might be wondering why I didn't want my father, Derek Sr., a former NFL player, to coach me. He actually did for a year when I was younger, but (sorry, Dad) I hated it. Honestly, I just wanted him to be sitting in the stands and cheering me on. And in high school, you could hear him yelling from the top of the bleachers, making sure that everyone in the stadium knew it was third down and his son was about to get a sack!

Over that summer, Derek Jr. and I committed to working out together every morning, starting at 5:00 a.m. Some days we would run up and down the water tower hill near my house, about a mile away from my high school. On one of the first days that we went, Derek Jr. made me run sprint after sprint until I was absolutely exhausted.

"That's enough, bro, I'm done!" I yelled at him. "I'm not doing these anymore!" I started to walk away.

"Once you quit one thing, you're a quitter for life!" he yelled back. I kept walking.

Derek Jr. was disappointed in me and didn't speak to me the rest of the day. All I kept hearing over and over in my head was him yelling, "Once you quit one thing, you're a quitter for life." I knew I was *not* a quitter, and I didn't *ever* want to be labeled that by anyone, especially my brother.

That night I made a promise to myself that I would never give anyone—including my brother—the satisfaction of letting them know they had gotten into my head and defeated or broken me. So the next day, I woke up at *4:30 a.m.*, thirty minutes before my brother did, and told him that I was ready to go.

He pushed and pushed me again, making me run more sprints than I had ever run in my life. My legs were shaking badly, but I didn't stop. He tried as hard as he could to break me, but this time I wouldn't let him. Whatever challenge he had for me, I met—without a single complaint. It was a life-changing day for me because I proved to him—but, more importantly, I proved to myself—that with a positive mindset, I could will myself to do anything I wanted to do.

That second day also gave me the confidence that I could push through any future hard times, which would include my recovery from my soon-to-come ACL, hip, and pec injuries.

Even today, when life comes at me fast and things aren't going my way, and I get that feeling like all I want to do is quit, my mind goes back to that hill, and I remember the positive mindset that I built. Then I use it to push forward.

Mindset Matters

It's important for me to have a positive mindset in order to do a good job on the field, to accomplish my financial goals, and to be a great husband and father. But what actually is a *mindset*? The concept is pretty easy to understand: it's what you believe about yourself, whether it's positive or negative. Those beliefs have a direct impact on your behavior.

Without a positive mindset, you can't move down the field toward your goals.

Without a positive mindset, you can't create the abundance that you want.

Without a positive mindset, you stop learning and growing.

Without a positive mindset, your motivation will stall, and your own negative self-talk will block you from becoming extraordinary.

Without a positive mindset, you will not achieve your own version of the American dream.

But, oh, mindsets are so much more than either positive or negative. Experts have broken it down further to include abundance mindset, learning mindset, fixed mindset, and even growth mindset, the latter means that you are open to learning and open to failure— and open to learning *from* failure. If you research mindset, you'll find about fifteen additional types, and every one of them is important in its own way. For instance, I know that I have a *growth* mindset because I always want to learn and improve myself, and of course, I always try to maintain a *positive* mindset. But what's the most important mindset that helps me to achieve my goals? It's called *intentional mindset.*

Intentional Mindset

Nutritionists tell us that eating a healthy breakfast is a great way to start your day. As an athlete, I agree, although I'll go one step further than that. Working on your mindset every morning is just as important as a great breakfast. Every morning, I set my intentions for the day by speaking out loud the three things I'm most grateful for and the three things I want to accomplish that day. Once I do that, everything I do is to honor and work toward those intentions.

It's important to note that goals and intentions are similar but not the same. When you set a goal in your life, it's one specific destination; when you set intentions, it's about direction. I like setting intentions rather than goals because you may not always hit a particular goal, but if you set intentions and make sure you are always heading in that direction, then you are putting yourself on the path to success. It all adds up.

God has given me gifts—physical, mental, emotional, and spiritual—and my daily *intention* is to maximize those gifts; once I do, I will continue to flip those bags that we talk about throughout the book. Every day, I wake up wanting to be the best that I can be for myself, God, my family, and my team.

In reading this book, you're also someone who wants to maximize your own gifts, talents, and skills that you've been given and also flip the bags, right? State those intentions every single day— they can change. If you do this, you will become more focused and ultimately achieve more than you ever have before. That's because you are now completely conscious of what you're working toward.

I started being intentional years ago, without even realizing it. When I was in the seventh grade, for example, we had an important basketball game against a rival team. I balled out and earned student-athlete-of-the-week honors. The school newspaper interviewed me and asked me about my goals in life.

"I want to go to USC, graduate, and play in the NFL," I stated matter-of-factly.

I knew what I wanted, and I said it out loud. The newspaper printed it, in black and white, for me and everyone else to see. My goal was to go to USC, graduate, and play in the NFL. That was now out there for the world to see. But what no one could see were the daily intentions I set, from middle school onward, that put me on a path to achieve those goals. Stating my intentions made me accountable and kept me focused on the bigger picture. To this day, a copy of that newspaper still hangs in my parents' house.

I'm a go-getter and absolutely relentless when it comes to achieving my goals, but it all starts by focusing on my mindset and setting my intentions. It should be the same for you. By setting your intentions, you can make sure your mindset embodies them.

How do you set intentions? It's fine to wake up and say, "I'm going to have a great day," but that's pretty generic. Change it to something more intentional and specific such as; "Today, I'm going to set a PR (personal record) on my deadlift, make an offer on a property I want to buy, and take my daughters to the park." This is much more focused. It provides you with action steps in order to achieve those goals. I always set my intentions in the car on my way to work. Then at the end of every day, I get on my knees and pray, then lay down in bed and reflect on whether I stayed true to my intentions for that day. You can take my tactic or create one of your own, like writing them down on cards or in your calendar. Figure out what works for you. You can have a great day but not even get off the couch. Notice, though, you can't achieve your deadlift PR or have fun at the park if you're sitting on the couch. But if your intention is, "I'm going to sit on the couch and read a book today," because it's something you don't do much of, then that's a great intention too.

Even NFL quarterback Tom Brady says that he plays with an intentional mindset. He once posted on his Instagram account, "Set the Intention, give it attention, allow for incubation, time the activation."

Negative Mindset

One type of mindset familiar to many of us often stands in the way of achieving our goals. That is a *negative mindset*.

This is when you or someone else says that you aren't good enough, or that you're a failure and you can't accomplish whatever it is you are trying to do. And the important part is that you *believe* it. Have you ever heard the quote, "Whether you say you can or you say you can't, you're right"? It's so true. A negative mindset will stop you from achieving whatever it is you want to achieve.

When I was on that hill that first time with my brother, I knew deep down that my body was capable of doing more, but I kept telling myself that I just couldn't do it. My body believed what my mind was telling it; sprinting suddenly became impossible. My negative mindset *literally* stopped me in my tracks, and I was the one in my own way. For me to get out of my own way, I had to change my mindset. Imagine if, before I went on the field each week, I said to myself, "Devon, you are not going to sack the QB!" Guess what probably would—or in this case, wouldn't—happen? Until you change what you're telling yourself about whatever situation you are in, and *believe what you can achieve*, things will remain status quo.

Maybe you are struggling with years of negative "I'm not good enough" self-talk. Perhaps you have been surrounded by toxic people who have sucked the wind out of your sails when you're trying to achieve your goals. Even parents are guilty of this, telling their children they shouldn't grow up to be something they themselves don't see as being successful. If this is the case for you, setting intentions and having a positive mindset probably does not come easy to you. In order to move forward, you need to hold off on flipping bags for now and work on flipping your mindset. Once you feel more confident, the bags will flip more easily for you.

Flip Your Mindset

To work on flipping your mindset, you need to find a tool to help you. This could include meditation, journaling, or some form of therapy. I have a daily habit of reading a very special notebook that I keep in my office. Inside are quotes I have written down that inspire, encourage, and uplift me. I've been adding quotes to this notebook for years, and I've even scattered some of my favorite ones around this book. I hope they motivate and focus you as much as they do me. Reading them regularly helps me stay positive and wipe out negativity. Since I never know what obstacles I will face on any given day, taking a few precious minutes to read these inspirational quotes is a great way to start my day. Sometimes I just open up the notebook to a random page and start reading. It never fails that I will find an encouraging word for whatever it is that I am going through in that moment.

Say It Strong

My notebook is not the only tool that I use to stay focused and positive.

I have been saying positive affirmations for years. I repeat the one right above to myself every day and do my best to live it. The whole idea of it came from wanting to maximize my mindset and be the best that I can be. I can't always control how my day plays out or what the outcome will be, and I might not always be the best player on the field, but I just want to know that I did the best that I could. I want to look in the mirror and be proud of the man that I'm looking at. Every day I want to glorify God, be relentless, and make sure I'm having fun. I'm working to be the best that I can be and controlling things that I can control.

Glorify God. Be relentless. Have fun.

Mike Tyson once said, "Everybody has a plan until they get punched in the mouth," and it's so true. I often set grand plans and intentions for my day, week, and month. More times than I would like to admit something goes wrong. I used to allow this to negatively impact me far too much. Now, thanks to "Glorify God. Be relentless. Have fun," I am able to stay focused and within myself.

Every day I ask myself, "Did I glorify God by doing the best I could with whatever circumstances were presented to me? Was I relentless in my pursuit of the things that I want? Did I make the most out of my situation and have fun?" Despite what happened that day, as long as I can say yes to these three questions, I know I am on the right track. By repeating this affirmation every day, I continue to develop into the best version of myself that I can be.

Here are more examples of my affirmations:

- I am highly favored and called to be great in all areas of my life.
- I am a relentless football player.
- I am more than an athlete and will be extremely successful outside of football.
- I will play ten-plus years in the NFL.
- I take care of myself physically, mentally, and emotionally.

I'm also happy to teach positive affirmations to my children. Every night, when I put my oldest daughter to bed, I have her repeat the following:

- I am strong!
- I am beautiful!
- I am smart!
- I can do anything!

A Carnegie Mellon study showed that even saying one brief self-affirmation is "effective in eliminating the harmful effects of chronic stress on problem-solving performance, such that chronically stressed self-affirmed participants performed under pressure at the same level as participants with low chronic stress levels."[1]

The easy thing about positive affirmations is that you can say them anywhere, at any time before, during, or after any situation in which you are involved. This could be before a big game or a test, a job interview, during an important meeting, or just because you need a boost of self-confidence at any given time.

So state an intention and say a positive affirmation or write it in a notebook or on your own bulletin board. It really makes a huge difference in how you approach your day and your life.

Be prepared to sacrifice what you are for what you will become.

Don't Listen to the Naysayers

When you are trying to achieve your goals, there are people who will do whatever they can to spoil it all.

Did you know that Walt Disney was fired from the *Kansas City Star* newspaper in 1919 because his editor said he *lacked imagination and had no good ideas?* Can you imagine if he had listened to his editor and questioned what would eventually become the genius of Disney?

Charles Darwin's own father called him *lazy* and *too dreamy*. Imagine how much of the earth you wouldn't know about if Darwin had believed his father? The good thing is that neither Disney nor Darwin listened to their naysayers—they might have *heard* them, but they didn't let it affect them. (Note: listening and hearing aren't the same thing. Listening is proactive, intentional; hearing is not.) Those two men knew who they were and what they could accomplish. As a result, they achieved an extraordinary amount of success in their lives.

Need more convincing? What about the Paralympians who might have been told they couldn't be athletes because of their disabilities? Yet they refused to believe what they were hearing and went on to compete in the Paralympics! Many win medals, and some of the elite Paralympians are incredible athletes who stack up well against elite able-bodied competitors. They had a positive mindset and blocked out the negativity to focus on their goals.

What about Venus and Serena Williams who worked hard to get out of Compton, California—a city known for its crime and gangs—and became two of the biggest tennis stars in the world? It all comes down to maximizing your mindset and stating your intentions.

When I was at USC, I had friends and teammates who would try to stop me from training or studying to instead go out with them and party. I often said no. Remember "popular Devon" from high school? I was a head honcho there, but in college I was different. I wasn't a party prude—I had friends, and I went out, but being popular and partying till all hours just didn't mean as much to me. It also wasn't worth what it would take to get myself back on track after being out late, especially during football season.

I had the self-confidence to know that my way of training hard and studying harder was the right way for *me*. I won't act like I was perfect with this though. I remember one night over the summer a few of my teammates and I went out, had a few too many drinks, and stayed up till 3:00 a.m. We had workouts scheduled for 6:00 a.m. Just my luck that the one time I let my guard down and stayed out late was followed up by mat drills, which is one of the hardest conditioning workouts that college strength coaches put you through. That was the last time I made that mistake. I must admit there were nights I had FOMO (fear of missing out), but I stayed true to what I believed, knowing that this was the best way to achieve my own goals.

Bouncing Back from a Loss

It's inevitable that we will lose some of our games, but some losses are harder to handle than others. Fast-forward to my career with the Arizona Cardinals (I signed with the Cardinals in March 2020, but more on that later). We started out the 2021 season strong, winning seven straight regular-season games. Heading into week 14, we were 10–3 and about to face the 1–11–1 Detroit Lions. Comparing the two teams on paper, it should have been an easy victory for us.

We lost, 30–12.

This loss was a great lesson about not resting on our laurels. Every NFL player needs to come to every game with the right mindset, ready to play with a level of humility, toughness, grit, and hard work. Just because the Lions had won only one of thirteen games before playing us didn't mean they were unable to beat us.

That being said, I hate losing. To deal with a loss, I try to maintain a short-term memory. Otherwise, if I hold on to a loss too long, it has way too much of an impact on my mindset and possibly my performance in next week's game. So I try to keep a level head and not get too high with the victories or too low with the losses.

When we lose, I become very analytical. If I missed a game-saving sack or interception or my team suffered a soul-crushing loss, I analyze what I could have done differently. How can I make sure that it won't happen again?

Every NFL team has either Monday or Tuesday off after a game, depending on each team's preference. If we aren't playing *Monday Night Football*, the Arizona Cardinals have Mondays off; on Tuesdays we watch film. Here we are very honest and transparent with ourselves about how we played as a defense and how we played as a team. We analyze everything and figure out what we need to improve on, what we need to keep doing, and what we need to let go of to move forward.

When something goes wrong in your business, how do you handle it? What things can you control, and what things can you not control? Let go of the things you cannot. For example, I play on defense and can't control what happens with the offense; the most I can do is encourage and talk to my offensive teammates if they aren't scoring. Beyond that, I need to be hyperfocused on what I can do on defense when I'm sent into the game. This is to reinforce within myself that I'm playing a role in stopping the other team's offense from scoring.

As I write this, our whole world is spinning because of a pandemic that has taken the lives of millions of people. Businesses have struggled, and many have closed for good. Individuals have lost jobs and homes. Maybe the pandemic (thankfully) didn't affect you financially and maybe you didn't lose your job, but maybe you find yourself thousands of dollars in debt. Maybe you are stuck in a nine-to-five job and can't seem to get your side hustle up and running. As a result, you are feeling defeated and like nothing is ever going to change.

Life is hard. At times like this, maximizing a positive mindset can be difficult, but you need to try. It might take time for your situation to change, but it *will* change if you stay focused.

If I'm Going to Fail . . .

It's common, even logical, to believe that sometimes we are going to fail at what we are trying to achieve. Here is what I tell myself about failure: "Let me do it on my terms. If I fail, I want to look back and know that I did everything I could. I want to know that if I failed, I did my absolute best and never wavered. If I fail, I want to look at myself in the mirror at night and still be proud of the man I see. If I fail, I want to know it's because of something I had absolutely no control over and it just wasn't in God's plans for me to accomplish, not because of things I can control."

So, if you're facing adversity, ask yourself, *What steps can I take to change the outcome the next time around?* What habits and skills can you bring to the table to improve your situation? What are the things that you can do to start implementing the right changes that will make a positive impact on your business?

_____

When nothing else is working,
work will work.

_____

Another Door Opens

Trade rumors and fans or media bashing me are examples of things beyond my control. I have had to grow a thick skin and just do the best I can. In unwanted circumstances such as those, I also become locked in on what I can control. I learned early on that life is going to throw me curveballs. If I get emotional and lose focus when we lose a game or even if I have a bad game in a game we win, or get bashed by the media, traded, or encounter other struggles in life, then it's even harder to do my best.

Truth be told, I wanted to stay with the New York Giants, but it just wasn't meant to be. I became a free agent after the 2017 season, and on March 15, 2018, I signed a three-year contract to play with the Detroit Lions. I was very fortunate because some NFL players do not get a second contract. They get drafted, play a few years and their career ends. But having several teams interested in me was validation of the way I had lived my life and the sacrifices I had made to get to this point.

Years ago, some people wondered if I would even make it into the NFL. I proved them wrong. Then there were those doubters who wondered if I would be relegated to special teams, then I won a starting spot. Sometimes it doesn't stop. Some then questioned if I was going to be one of those players who played for only a few years, but I surpassed that. In becoming a second-contract guy with the Lions, I really felt like I made it. I stayed true to myself. I worked really, really hard. I had built resiliency and had the right mindset to go with it.

But when I was a kid, my goal wasn't to just "make it" to the NFL. My goal was to have a long career in the NFL, become a respected player, and, of course, make enough money to take care of my family.

Some well-meaning people likely believed that if my career had ended with the New York Giants, I should have been happy with the consolation of playing a couple years in the NFL and banking some money. That wasn't me; I wanted more. Signing a second contract with another team was the validation I wanted and worked hard for. And for me, it was just the beginning.

Once I signed with the Detroit Lions, I created new goals, like making it to ten years in the NFL and achieving even higher financial goals in my investments and businesses.

Next, I worked hard for the respect of my Lions teammates, and on September 9, 2018, they voted me team captain. That further inspired me. One week later, during a game against the San Francisco 49ers, I recorded four combined tackles and made two sacks on 49ers' quarterback Jimmy Garoppolo (although we lost).

Off the field, my focus turned to making enough mailbox money that if I stopped playing football at any point, my family and I would be taken care of. I wanted to generate enough mailbox money so that I could retire from football and our lifestyle would not have to change at all. I had grown my real estate investment portfolio substantially. I was able to keep earning money while having extra coming in to reinvest in new deals.

I had a dream just like you probably have a dream. If you love technology, your dream might be to work for IBM or Microsoft. Let's say you get hired by IBM. In such a case you probably would continue to prove yourself and work your way up the corporate ladder. You'll be given regular reviews about the job that you're doing, and you will learn about things you are doing well and the areas in which you need to improve. Constructive criticism is good, even if your first reaction to hearing it is disappointment. Constructive criticism can identify for you your weaknesses or deficiencies you might not be able to see yourself. It is that way for everybody. Live with it; grow from it; excel because of it.

You'll need to keep a positive mindset so you can get to where you want to go. This is no different than what happened to me in the NFL. I got drafted and I *still* had to prove myself and keep my positive mindset. I signed a new deal with Detroit, but then I had to prove myself again and show that I was worthy of that contract (spoiler alert—I *never* stop having to prove myself). The Detroit

Lions wanted *me*, so it was time to pack my bags again and take all that I've learned to the Motor City. I was about to become extraordinary on a whole new level.

 Before you can flip the bag, you must flip your mindset. If your mind can conceive it, then you can achieve it!

CHAPTER SEVEN

Become Extraordinary

It's never been about what you got.
It's more about what you do with what you got.

Wㅤhen I was playing for the New York Giants we ran a 4–3
ㅤㅤscheme on defense, and I was our Sam linebacker. (In case
you didn't know it, the Sam, Mike, and Will linebackers are the
primary linebackers in a 4–3 scheme, and the names describe the
positions: "Mike" is often the middle linebacker; "Will" is the weak-
side linebacker, and "Sam" is the strong-side linebacker.)

Our defensive coordinator, Steve Spagnuolo, recognized that I
was good at playing on the line of scrimmage, so he installed an
under defense that allowed the defensive end to move inside to
what we call a 5 technique and me to play on the edge. So that's
where I played, rather than off the ball, as a true linebacker in many
4–3 schemes. But even though I played on the line of scrimmage,
I didn't have many opportunities to rush the quarterback; most of
my time was spent in pass coverage. Fortunately, with the few
chances I did get in those first two seasons to rush the passer, Spags

recognized my natural ability. So he let me play as our extra pass rusher in third-down situations during my third and fourth years on the team. Over four seasons, I ended up earning nine and a half sacks on limited pass-rushing snaps. It wasn't bad but I knew I could do better. In other words, I wanted to be *extraordinary*.

So I decided to invest in *me*.

Warren Buffett once said, "Investing in yourself is the most important investment you'll ever make in your life. There's no financial investment that'll ever match it because if you develop more skill, more ability, more insight, more capacity, that's what's going to really provide economic freedom.... It's those skill sets that really make that happen."

Me, Master Joe Kim, and my brother after a training session
Photo credit: Devon Kennard

After I became a free agent in the off-season after the 2017 season, I didn't know where I would end up. What I did know was that I wanted to be part of a team that would give me an opportunity to pass rush more. Keeping that in mind, I reached out to Master Joe Kim and paid him to fly out to Arizona. Kim now works for the New England Patriots, but at the time he was a freelance specialist coach who has had an extensive and successful career coaching and improving the performances of multiple NFL pass rushers. Of course I wanted him to train me on pass rushing.

By using a unique combination of film study and football drills, we worked on enhancing my skills. The footwork, hand placement, and body mechanics he taught me really took my game to the next level. For instance, until now I had never paid attention to the number of steps I took before I threw a move. After some film study, he pointed out that my most effective moves happened when I was on my third step. This led me to start playing from a two-point stance with my inside leg up. This way my outside foot was my third step, and I could throw my move and beat the offensive tackle.

Okay, now hang with me as I explain some technique stuff here. Pushing my pass rush moves up the field three big steps and then throwing my move put me in position to have a two-way go (a choice) on the offensive lineman depending on how fast back he set. If he did not kick far enough back by the time I hit my third step, I could beat him around the edge. If he sets too far back, I could push him by and go underneath. If he set the perfect amount, that's when I could use power, bull-rush him, and make him lean one way or another before I took an edge. It seems simple now, but understanding this made such a difference in my game!

The investment was worth it. Over the next *two* seasons with the Lions, I landed fourteen sacks—almost double the total of what I had in the four seasons I was with the Giants.

Signing my contract with the Detroit Lions
Photo credit: Detroit Lions

Years ago someone said to me, "Complacency is the cousin to death," and I didn't want to be the one responsible for killing my NFL career. Instead, I worked even harder to become *extraordinary* before I even knew where I would land.

I made the conscious decision to invest in myself—hiring Joe Kim—to improve my skills, and it paid off. In addition to enhancing my pass rushes, I became the first linebacker in Lions history to record at least forty tackles and five sacks in multiple seasons. I also had single-season career highs with forty-five solo tackles, fifteen QB hits, and two fumble recoveries while matching career bests with fifty-eight total tackles and seven sacks in 2019.

Real Estate Extraordinaire

I applied the very same principles of becoming extraordinary on the football field to my financial endeavors. I needed to continue learning and put the pieces into place so my investments would provide me with financial stability once I hung up my cleats for good.

After getting my feet wet with the Indiana home I had bought (which I covered back in chapter 2), I sold it and made a return of better than 125 percent on my investment. Not bad for my first experience in real estate investing.

During my time with the Lions, I purchased twelve units in Kansas City and six single-family homes in Ohio—all with cash. My plan was to hold on to these properties and generate up to $15,000 a *month* in mailbox money. That would be enough for my family and me to live off comfortably every year without changing our lifestyle at all. Plus we would still have extra money to continue investing in more properties.

Speaking of becoming extraordinary, my wife, Camille, who managed dental offices by trade, changed careers after we got married. She dedicated herself to becoming an exceptional real estate agent in Arizona. As I write this, we have already purchased two investment properties here—one long-term rental and one short-term rental—and we're collaborating to find even more investment properties. Real estate is priced *much* higher in Arizona compared to the average of $100,000 I was spending per property in the Midwest, so our strategy has had to be different. For instance, in the Midwest I was able to buy turnkey properties that were cash-flowing right away. I got so used to that I thought I could use the same strategy everywhere and quickly realized turnkey properties in Arizona did not have cash flow as well if at all. This has presented a unique challenge for my wife and me, but we are excited to grow our real estate knowledge and build our portfolio in our home state.

How You Can Become Extraordinary

Don't skip over this section because you think you don't have it in you. No skipping keys allowed! No matter what your circumstances are—if you are in a corporate job or are a budding entrepreneur— you have the ability to go from ordinary to extraordinary. Everyone does. Remember what I said in the last chapter—if you think you *can* or you think you *can't*, both are true. So why not choose *can* and become great at whatever it is you do!

But first, what does becoming extraordinary even mean? It means consistently working harder and improving your skill set, going beyond what's mandatory, and doing what's necessary to take yourself to the next level in your life and career. *Everyone* does what's mandatory. Most people go to work and do at least the minimum required at their job so they don't get fired. Being extraordinary means going to work and doing more than what is required. It might mean showing up early or staying a little later, learning a new skill that can help your team, coming up with new ideas, and working efficiently.

Ask yourself, "Am I doing the bare minimum or am I finding ways to go beyond that and do what's necessary for me to become the best I can be?" Maximize your potential in whatever it is you are pursuing, which in turn helps you flip the bag.

Earlier I asked you to write down *your* version of the American dream as well as your vision. If your vision is to launch a product that you invented, you need to hustle. That means using your time off to sell your product and let as many potential customers know that they *need* your product. It means using your time off to build a social media buzz in order to create publicity and reach out to vendors and stores.

The harder you work, the more opportunities you have for your sales to increase. Then one day you will have sold enough of your product to generate enough cash flow to hand in your letter of resignation. Believe in that and expect it. Once you can focus on your new business full time, you'll make even more money and can leverage this success into additional income and opportunities. You will have achieved your version of the American dream. But first you need to achieve key 2—*you need to become extraordinary.*

Maybe you don't want to leave your current job because you love what you do. Yet at the same time you want to make more money, get out of debt, and create a solid financial future. You need management to notice you. How? Ask for more responsibilities. Learn new skills. Volunteer for something. Come up with an idea that can help streamline your company's business or practices or even just your job, and show them. When you go above and beyond like this, you will see that your earning potential is bolstered.

Improving your current skill set is the step that a lot of people skip. This adds value to you as an employee or as a business owner. Adding value allows you to make more money. Making more money will improve your financial situation, and this will catapult you to the next level of your financial dreams.

Winners Do Have Systems

A sign on the bulletin board in my home office says, "Losers have goals, winners have systems." I have many systems—some people call them habits—for each important thing in my life. Right now those important things are faith, family, football, finances, and philanthropy.

So what are my systems? For my faith and relationship with God, I make sure to pray every night with my oldest daughter before she goes to bed. I also read a Bible verse on my own every morning. I go to chapel every week, and on game day, I listen to an online sermon.

When it comes to my family, I'm very mindful of the time that I spend with my wife and children when I'm at home. After my oldest daughter's gymnastics class every week, I pick her up and follow our Chick-fil-A routine, which is to get her her favorite chicken nuggets. It's our special time that fits together into our day and means a lot to me. My wife and I have dates every Friday. That's our day to spend quality time together.

In football, my system is to take care of my body by getting treatment twice a week, doing extra cardio a few times a week, and getting massages twice a week. This is all on top of our regular practice schedule. It's predictable, but it's disciplined and it's a system that works for me.

So what's important to you and how can you build your own systems for each? From reading this book, you should have a great idea of what *your* American dream looks like so far. Based on your dream, I hope you have some goals you hope to reach and set intentions to reach those goals. The next step is to take that information and create systems for every major aspect in your life—as I mentioned earlier, for me that is faith, family, football, finances, and philanthropy—make sure the systems you create for every aspect in your life align with the life you ultimately want. Once you set these systems do *not* get bored with consistency. Execute these systems regularly, and you will begin to see a change for the better. It all adds up.

For example, finances should be on your list, so what systems can you implement to help move your financial goals forward? Can you spend an hour every day, or at minimum once a week, reading personal finance books or listening to financial podcasts? Can you dedicate time to reviewing your spending, saving, and investing habits and then devising or finding ways you can improve them? Carve time into your schedule.

Some people start a system that they cannot maintain, so I must remind you that doing *something* is better than nothing. Start small. If you currently do not spend any time on your finances, start by scheduling thirty minutes once a week and build from there. I promise it will become a habit and begin to make a difference.

You can keep coming up with reasons or excuses about what is stopping you from becoming extraordinary. If you want to achieve something badly enough, however, *nothing* will stop you—you will start doing what's necessary for you to get there. But just in case, let's address some of the things that might be standing in your way:

Think you're too young?
During the pandemic and quarantine, a friend of mine told me about her daughter, Sami, who had just graduated from college. Sami was working at a fast-food restaurant during breaks and summers for extra money while she studied photography. She really wanted to leave her fast-food job, but the pandemic forced businesses to close their doors to customers, and there was an all-around hiring freeze. Sami knew this was not the time to make a change, so she decided to stay put at her job. She decided this even though she had her diploma in hand and was itching to get her photography career off the ground. She had bills to pay, and because fast-food workers were considered essential workers, she was almost certain

her job was secure. That security of a paycheck was vital during the pandemic.

But Sami wasn't complacent about her job. Instead, she made certain to not miss any shifts and covered for her coworkers when they couldn't come in. She offered to work the less-popular closing shifts. All of her efforts were noticed by the higher-ups, and her manager gave her a large bonus for all of her hard work. But it wasn't just what she was doing at the restaurant that was impressive. What she did in her downtime was even more remarkable.

Sami used her time at home during quarantine to research local exhibitions to which she could submit her photographs. This would give her opportunities to have her work showcased and a chance to earn extra income. Within the year, Sami's photographs had been accepted by *eight* local exhibitions—some virtually and some in-person for when visitors were again allowed in to roam the galleries checking out the creative work like Sami's. Along the way, she won cash awards and honorable mentions. Her photographs were also accepted to an exhibition in Rome, Italy!

Sami's other goal was to get hired by a local photography studio whose work she admired. They finally posted an opening and Sami's impressive résumé stood out. When the time was right, she got the job and left her fast-food position behind. Sami was extraordinary during a very difficult time in the world. With her skills, positive mindset, and can-do attitude, she's on her way to becoming an extremely successful photographer.

You can learn a lot about becoming extraordinary by watching *Shark Tank*, a television show where entrepreneurs pitch "sharks," or wealthy investors, in order to get them to invest in their product or service. Watching the show you'll see and hear about entrepreneurial innovators who are *all-in* with whatever product they invented or service they devised. Many of these entrepreneurs have overcome tremendous obstacles to achieve their success and get on the show, and it can be an emotional experience for everyone involved—not just those pitching but also the viewers and even the sharks at times. These hard chargers have spent countless hours trying to sell their product or get it into retail stores. They have invested their own money, and some have sacrificed almost everything in the name of their goals. Many entrepreneurs have become extraordinary before they even stepped in front of the sharks, and now they want to take it to a whole new level.

One of the most popular sharks on the show is Mark Cuban, who is also the owner of the NBA's Dallas Mavericks. He knows what it was like to be in their shoes. When Cuban was only twelve years old, he started selling garbage bags door to door. He went on to create MicroSolutions, a computer consulting service and, after a few years, sold it for millions. He then created Broadcast.com and ultimately sold that for $5.6 *billion*. It all started with garbage bags.

Think you're too broke?

You don't need a lot of money to become extraordinary. In some cases, you don't even need *any* money. With just $700, John DeJoria started John Paul Mitchell hair products. Shutterstock was developed by an amateur photographer looking to make some extra cash, so he uploaded extra photographs he had that others could use. Jan Koum, who created WhatsApp, came from poverty in Ukraine and used his downtime to learn about computers. He was then hired by Yahoo and leveraged his knowledge of the app industry to start his own business in 2009. He sold it in 2014 to Facebook for $19 billion. Dell Computers was started in Michael Dell's college dorm with only a $1,000 loan.

Think you're not good enough?

In Will Smith's autobiography, *Will*, he tells the story of when he was in high school and started rapping. He had a natural ability and was good at freestyling. No one, however, including his own mother, thought it had a chance at becoming a legit money-making profession. Well, Will did. He did whatever he needed to do to prove everyone wrong. In the 1990s, rap music was raw and uncut, with cussing and lyrics about drugs and violence. Will ignored the noise and made the decision not to cuss in his raps. His music was called "corny," and most thought he would never make it in the rap game. The odds were stacked against him.

Will doubled down and devoted even more time and energy to become extraordinary, which led him to winning four Grammys! Will's story is a great reminder that if you stay true to yourself and put the work in, you are good enough to accomplish anything you want to!

Think you're too short/tall/big/small?

Kyler Murray, my teammate and quarterback for the Arizona Cardinals, is listed as five feet ten and is considered one of the shortest quarterbacks, if not *the* shortest, in the NFL right now. I remember when he was in college how football scouts said he was too short to play QB. Despite that, he ended up winning the Heisman Trophy, given to the best college football player in America, while at Oklahoma. Then, while Kyler was getting ready for the NFL Draft, college football pundits criticized him, saying, for instance, that his hands were too small and he was too short and therefore wouldn't be able to throw over the line of scrimmage in the NFL.

Despite all of this, Kyler has proved to be one of the best young quarterbacks in the NFL. In just three years, he has helped turn the

Arizona Cardinals organization around and into a real Super Bowl contender.

Kyler isn't the only one who has had to overcome physical limitations. Who can forget the Philadelphia Eagles' Darren Sproles, who was one of the best punt returners and third-down running backs ever to play in the NFL. Sproles is only five feet six, which is considered *very* short for the NFL. When I was with the New York Giants, I played against Darren a lot when he was with the Eagles, and I can tell you that his size was actually his *advantage*!

Vince Wilfork is a six-foot-two, 330-pound former nose tackle who played in the NFL for thirteen seasons, primarily with the New England Patriots. If you ever saw him in person, you would not think a man that large could be the caliber athlete that he was; but he defied all logic. By the end of his career, he had a highlight reel full of extraordinary plays!

Remember, it's not the size of the dog in the fight but the size of the fight in the dog, so do not let your physical limitations box you in and stop you from accomplishing your dreams.

Think your circumstances are hard?

Before she became an Oscar-winning actress, Halle Berry revealed to *People* magazine that she had spent time in a homeless shelter when she was only twenty-one and trying to break into show business. "I took my modeling money, and I thought, 'Oh, I've got some cash!' When you get to New York . . . three months later I was out of my cash and called my mother to ask her to send me some money, but she said no. That's probably one of the best things she did for me because it taught me. She said, 'If you want to be there, then you be there. You work it out.' And I had to work it out. You say I can't? Watch me. I'm going to figure this out. And shelter life was part of figuring it out for a minute."

And how about Jay-Z? These days, he owns real estate, art, and Tidal,[1] and he has the baddest chick in the game now, but Jay-Z actually grew up in a housing project in Brooklyn, New York. Think about that. That's where there were just as many wannabe rappers as there were crack dealers, and he was both. He didn't let his humble beginnings squash his dreams. At twenty-seven years old, he and two of his friends founded record label Roc-A-Fella Records. The same year, Jay-Z released his first album, *Reasonable Doubt*.

Nipsey Hussle, one of my favorite rappers, joined South Central gangs in order to survive before he became a success in the music industry. Before his tragic death, Hussle overcame his past to inspire young Black men and denounce gun violence through his music, influence, and community work. Sadly, Hussle was shot and killed a day before he was to meet with LAPD officials to address gang violence in South Los Angeles. The thirty-three-year-old left a mark on those who think that you can't escape a rough past and become extraordinary at something you want to do.

These are great examples of people who have overcome adversities to become extraordinary, but now it's your time to do the same. Remember, "It's not about what you got, but what you do with what you got." It's about being *extraordinary* with what you've been blessed with and flipping your bag.

The more value you add to yourself the more extraordinary you will become. As you become more extraordinary, flipping the bag becomes easier. Greatness is rewarded!

CHAPTER EIGHT

Monetize Your Passions

Follow your own passion—not anyone else's but *yours*!

The best feeling in the world is getting paid to do what you love. So, what do you love to do? What are you passionate about? I'm asking what *you* are passionate about, not what your parents, family, or friends think you should be passionate about! I'm not asking what your coach wants you to do, and I am definitely not asking what your major was in college or what you feel obligated to do.

In this day and age, there are more ways to profit from your passion than ever before. You don't even have to quit your current job or bank a bunch of money before you start doing what it is that you love to do. Right now, right this very minute, you can start to make money doing what you love to do!

Football became a profitable career for me, but it hasn't been my *only* passion. Obviously, I became passionate about real estate investing, but at one point it was only a dream that I would ever make money off of it. It took some time, but I was happy that I didn't have to wait until I retired from the NFL to make money investing in real estate. And whatever it is that *you* want to do, you do not need to wait either. As a matter of fact, the sooner you start, the sooner you can start getting closer to your dreams.

Split the Difference

It's important to understand the difference as well as the overlap between *monetizing your passion* and *earning mailbox money* (which I introduced in chapter 2 and will talk about again in chapter 10). Quick review: mailbox money is earning money on a regular basis with little to no effort on your part. Monetizing your passion means making money doing something that you love to do. Monetizing your passion *can* lead to earning mailbox money, but that's not *always* the case.

On the other hand, when you are creating mailbox money it doesn't automatically mean you are monetizing a passion.

For example, if I'm hired as a keynote speaker for an event and I'm paid a fee, that fee is *not* mailbox money. It is a one-time fee for my service, not recurring mailbox money. It is however, monetizing my passion because I love speaking in front of people about football, personal finance, and real estate. Again, getting paid for what I love to do.

Now here's where it gets a little tricky. Writing this book is a one-time event, but sales of it can go on indefinitely (I hope). If I sell the book while I'm giving a keynote speech and the sales continue after the conference is over, that qualifies as mailbox money because it, again hopefully, keeps coming on a regular basis.

Ideally, you should find ways where monetizing your passion also creates regular mailbox money, although let's not forget the basic premise of monetizing your passion is simply to make money doing the things that you enjoy. Not only will you be happier because you're doing what you love to do, but you can build a financial cushion that will open up even more opportunities.

The Hows

Now that you know the benefits of monetizing your passions, *how* do you actually make money? Here are just a few ideas to get you started:

Share your knowledge: No matter what it is that you are passionate about—dogs, furniture, jewelry, video games, sports, or comic books—you can share what you know with others by starting a blog, website, vlog, or an educational course. For example, let's say that you love art design. On websites like Fiverr, you can post your skills for hire, set your own fees, and start making money working from anywhere in the world. Say you have a passion for video games, and you are great at a game like *Fortnite* or *Overwatch*. There are kids who make millions of dollars by letting people watch them play on applications such as Twitch. According to streamerfacts .com, small streamers make anywhere from $50 to $1,500 per month depending on the number of average viewers that they have. Big streamers make anywhere from $5,000 to $30,000 per month.

Create a YouTube channel: Once you have a YouTube channel and have gained a number of followers, you can start to get paid to have businesses advertise on your channel. There are people who make thousands of dollars on videos they posted years ago! The chance to record a video one time and make money on that video for years in the future is something that many people are taking advantage of right now.

By the time this book comes out, I will have debuted my own YouTube channel, using it to discuss a lot about topics from this book. YouTube is another revenue stream, but it's a little different when it comes to earning mailbox money. First, to be successful on this platform—and pretty much any social media—you need to consistently produce new content to grow an audience.

That takes work, but what is great is that a video I post today on YouTube can still generate mailbox money for me one, three, or even five years from now. I look at it this way: I have to do the work now but can benefit from this work for a long time.

I created a setup in my office where I can easily record videos. I bought a camera, lighting, and audio equipment. This makes it relatively easy for me to press play on my camera anytime I have a topic that is worth talking about. I record the video and post it online. Presto! That freshly produced video lives on, theoretically, forever on my YouTube channel. If I post one video a week that takes five minutes to record, I will soon have a growing compilation of self-created videos that will allow me to gradually build what early on is a small audience into a large YouTube following, and then revenue from advertisers drawn to my YouTube channel will follow. My goal is to work one hour a week on YouTube; that one hour stacked with all the ones that came before and those that will follow could potentially lead to millions of dollars of revenue from those paid advertisements. It's all about attracting increasingly more eyeballs to my video content, which in turns ramps up advertising revenue, and now I have a side business scaling to new heights. In this case I can monetize my passion using YouTube, but it can ultimately turn into a mailbox generator over time as well.

Now, to be honest, it takes time to make money on YouTube, unless you have a video that goes viral. But if you love doing it, stick to it, and look for creative ways to bring in sponsors or get paid to create a video, it can become a lucrative way to monetize your passion.

Sponsors and paid subscribers: Do you already run a blog in your spare time and now you want to focus on it full time? Find sponsors for ads on your site or offer a paid subscriber option in which you give subscribers bonus content that is not offered to regular readers of your site. You can also offer affiliate-marketing links in your posts. Affiliate links are where you make commissions on sales of products that you recommended. Write about them on your blog or mention them on your podcast and provide a link to where readers can buy the product. Each time a reader or listener clicks on the affiliate link and purchases the product, you earn a commission from the company.

Invest: Invest in companies that you are passionate about and that align with your core values. For instance, I have friends who love electric cars, so they have invested in Tesla and some of the other electric car manufacturers. I know others who are avid crypto fans and have a large portion of their portfolio invested in that space.

Sell products: Do you paint or are you a clothing designer? Do you take photographs? You can upload your work to sites such as Etsy or Søciety6 and sell calendars, clothing, tote bags, and more with your products all from the comfort of your own home.

Start a business: I met a man who loves being out on the water so much that he bought a boat and charges a premium to take groups of people out every day. He took me and my family out on Lake Pleasant in Arizona. To no one's surprise, he has built a lucrative business taking guests on his boat.

Be creative: Guy Fieri is a world-renowned food taster. He began his journey on the Food Network by winning the second season of *The Next Food Network Star*. He was granted his own show, *Guy's Big Bite*, which then launched several incredibly successful shows including *Diners, Drive-Ins and Dives* (aka *Triple D*). On *Triple D*, Fieri travels all over America visiting and featuring various restaurants and trying their food, while getting paid by the Food Network to do it. Launching your career by entering a contest is a great way to monetize your passion if you win.

No matter what you are passionate about, there is a way to monetize it. I can almost guarantee that you can find someone else who is already doing what you love; but know there is plenty of room out there for competitors. Why not you? Never assume that there are others just like you who have a head start doing and making lots of money from "your" idea, when in fact there are many more people like you *not* taking that first step that you are now contemplating. Go for it! No more waiting around. If you don't take that chance and start working on things that will help you monetize your passion, it won't happen for you. Sitting on your thumbs afraid to step out is not a good business strategy. But if you are willing to take a shot and start that business, create that course, post that content, or whatever it is for you, then you are finally starting the journey and giving yourself a chance to make money doing what you love. Maybe your business doesn't explode into instant wealth, and it rarely does. Just go with it and stick with it.

Once you start, stay consistent and be adaptable. Just because you took a shot and started your clothing line, doesn't mean you will immediately be profitable. You will need to put in time and energy every day to get to the point where it's lucrative.

Almost all the time I am either evaluating or already underwriting (financing) properties that I'm interested in buying. It's tedious work that's not always fun, but it's necessary for pursuing my real estate goals. For that reason alone I never really mind doing the work. My other passion is public speaking about financial literacy, personal development, and real estate. I am working with my marketing team to build a section of my business that allows me to do more of that.

What can you be doing to do the same? What's your idea? I bet it's a good one, or at least better than perhaps you even realize. You won't know unless you take the plunge. Getting all wet isn't a bad thing. Just towel yourself off and go again. Who knows? That next plunge might be into a pool full of cash.

Leveraging Social Media

In 2022, I had fifty-seven thousand followers on Instagram and twenty-four thousand followers on Twitter. NFL players with millions of followers include the likes of quarterbacks such as Russell Wilson and Patrick Mahomes and wide receivers such as Odell Beckham Jr., not guys like me who are typically on defense and not marquee players on their team. But if there's one thing I've learned, it's that social media is about leveraging those numbers into profit. Even accounts with only a thousand followers can make money.

Some platforms, like TikTok and Instagram, require a minimum number of followers and/or likes before they will pay you in cash for all this attention that you're getting. It can become a regular way to make mailbox money, but with fewer followers, you can still gain the attention of brands that want to pay you to do sponsored posts, review their products, or work with them in some way that rolls over to you as financially beneficial. It's about *engagement*.

For example, let's say that you have 965 followers on Instagram. Your competition has more than five thousand. You might be wondering "Why bother?" but every post you put up averages two hundred likes with 965 followers, while your competition averages fifty likes with more than five thousand. Guess who's generating more interest here? That's not a trick question—*you*, of course. Your engagement rate is higher, so brands might be interested in working with you more than with your competitor because your posts reach more of their potential buyers.

Sometimes you just have to dig a little deeper.

I've leveraged my years in the NFL and my social media presence into money-making brand deals, such as the ones I made with Kia and, most recently, Lincoln.

The 2005 Kia Sorento that I had shipped to New York when I was with the Giants was a gift from my parents to me. I drove it for two and a half years of high school, all five years I was at USC, and my first year in the NFL. In 2014, toward the end of my rookie year, during the Northeast's bitterly cold winter, I started having issues with it. I took it to a New Jersey Kia dealership for maintenance, and while I was there, I built a relationship with the owner.

We worked out a unique marketing deal in which I would post on my social media about driving a brand new Kia Cadenza, and they would pay my monthly car payments. Not a bad deal, huh? I was driving the vehicle for free just like Eli Manning did with his Toyota! It was the first marketing deal that I constructed on my own, and I accomplished it by walking into the dealership and treating people well. I then coupled that with my social media presence. The next thing I knew I was driving a new car for free. It's another great example of how networking can be beneficial to your success. Although I didn't earn money on this arrangement, I wasn't paying any for the car either. For the next three years, I drove the Cadenza and shipped my Sorento back to Arizona, where I drove it in the off-season.

In 2021, I was approached by Lincoln with a money-making opportunity—drive an Aviator, take pictures of me with it, and post it on my social media. The arrangement required me to post four times on my social media pages and six Instagram stories. In return, I was given the car for six months and paid a healthy fee. The arrangement was easy, but I went over and beyond what they asked me to do. I hired a professional photographer to take a variety of high-quality photos of me in different outfits and wrote well-thought-out posts that I published over several days.

Me with the Lincoln Aviator
Photo credit: Askia Stewart Jr. for Lincoln Photo

All that mattered to Lincoln was that more than fifty thousand people were going to see a photo on my Instagram account of me driving their car. My goal was for Lincoln to again work with me sometime in the future because of how hard I had worked for them. Remember when earlier in the book I said that you need to be extraordinary at your passions before you can monetize them? Being extraordinary should continue even *after* you monetize.

Just to clarify, I do not put content on my social media accounts just to attract deals or to follow trends. I share content that matches my professional goals and represents the direction in which I want my career to go. I believe that because I've stayed authentic to who I am on my social media accounts, the opportunities coming to me will continue to multiply while my followers increase.

There are more than a *billion* active users on Instagram alone. That might make your head spin, but don't lose focus. Instead, keep the presence of mind to ask yourself how to stand out from your competition in order to gain followers, generate publicity, and make sales. Greatness is not hard to reach. It's about doing the simple things really well.

It all adds up.

Inspiration

WWE professional wrestler Stone Cold Steve Austin was known for slamming two beers together in the ring and guzzling them down. Years later, he took his passion for brew and started his own IPA, launching Broken Skull IPA in 2014 in collaboration with El Segundo Brewing Co. of Southern California. According to the *Los Angeles Times*, the brewery could ferment sixty barrels at a time before the wrestler walked in. That skyrocketed to 580 the following year, and in 2018, EL Segundo Brewing sold 5,700 barrels. In 2019 they sold more than 7,000 barrels. All because Stone Cold said so.

Musical icon Rihanna, born Robyn Fenty, started her life as a poor girl in Barbados with an alcoholic and abusive father before becoming an extremely successful recording artist. But as much as her songs "Umbrella," "Loyalty," and "Diamonds" rocked her into the stratosphere, she has found even more success with her other passions: beauty and fashion. She launched her makeup line Fenty Beauty, lingerie line Savage X Fenty, and luxury fashion brand Fenty, which have made her a billionaire and the wealthiest woman in the world next to Oprah Winfrey.

Michael Strahan, another man I respect and admire, is another great example of monetizing his passion. He is an NFL Hall of Fame defensive end who shares the single-season sack record (twenty-two and a half), but as soon as he retired from the NFL, he leveraged his natural gift for public speaking, hosting, and interviewing to become one of the most recognizable faces on TV. He didn't undergo a makeover or reinvent himself—he was always prepping himself for life after football.

DEVON DEBUNKS

I'm sure you've heard the motto, "Follow your passion and the money will follow" a few times, but beware: that statement is very misleading. It should be, "Follow your passion and money *can* follow." Just because you are following your passion does not mean you will automatically fulfill your American dream and make enough money to ride off into the sunset. If that were the case, wouldn't more people be satisfied in this world? The reality is that you have to be willing to do the work for it. Money just doesn't follow you. Keep in mind, though, that simple willingness to do what needs to be done separates you from the pack.

This is why I titled this chapter "*Monetize* Your Passions." *Following* your passion and *monetizing* your passion are *not* the same thing. You can be the greatest NFT creator in the world (NFT is short for "nonfungible token," a type of financial security consisting of digital data) but if you do not know how to market them, you can have some awesome-looking NFTs that are worth virtually nothing. In the meantime, your competitor has done the work, marketing and building a community around their NFT brand that has made them millions.

A good example of this is CryptoPunks. I have come across many NFT collectibles that look *way* cooler (in my opinion) than CryptoPunks but aren't worth even a fraction of what a Crypto-Punk is worth. CryptoPunk creators created a community that felt exclusive, and that exclusivity made people want to be a part of it. It became cool to say you owned a CryptoPunk. They had a plan from the start and executed it well, which led them to becoming one of the most desired NFTs in 2021 and 2022. So the difference between following your passion and monetizing your passion is that one *might* lead to profit while the other one *will* lead to profit.

One of the greatest feelings in the world is when you start making money doing something you love. The first dollar is usually the hardest one to make so don't give up!

CHAPTER NINE

Network Your Way to Success

Purposeful networking can increase the quality
of your life and deepen your pockets.

Looking back at everything that I have accomplished, I can honestly say that I couldn't have done any of it without networking.

On my first day at USC I heard these five words: "The Trojan family is real." We pride ourselves on this mantra. You can go to *any* university for four years, but when you're a Trojan, it's for life. And boy, were they right. The importance of networking started when I walked onto that campus, and many of the Trojans that I met really did become family for me and still are, even years later.

I took advantage of every networking opportunity that the school had. I wanted to build relationships—with the boosters and alumni, for example—because I knew that they might be in a position to help me down the line with their knowledge and experiences. Going to USC and making it my goal to network once I got there completely changed my life for the better. It's been a decade since I graduated, and I still have maintained dozens of USC connections and relationships. I'm also regularly invited to speak on campus, which is something I love to do.

I developed a network of relationships that have been financially beneficial to me long after I left. If you graduate college with just a diploma and a mountain of debt, you didn't do it right. If you're still in college, you can change your destiny right now.

Networking is about working smarter, not harder. It's also about showing people that you're interested in them, what they're talking about, what they do, and what their interests are. When you do, you automatically stand out from the crowd, and that benefits you as you work toward your goals.

Business Cards Still Matter

Before I learned about real estate, I thought about a career in broadcasting or getting a regular corporate job after I left the NFL. Yet I really wasn't sold on any one profession. I just knew I wanted to be successful, so I made it a point at these USC networking events to ask people about their careers.

After striking up a conversation with someone I've just met, and if I am interested in their career path or believe he or she can add value to my life in some way, I do everything I can to continue the relationship. I start by asking for their business card. When I get home, I write down as much as I can remember about each person and then input their contact information into my phone. Then, here is the unique part: I pick four random dates over the next year and put a reminder on my calendar to reach out to that person. When that date comes, I go to their contact on my phone, read the notes I wrote, and write a thoughtful note to them.

For example, someone I met told me that their favorite thing to do is go on an annual trip with their son. When I reach out, this becomes my first talking point.

"It was nice meeting you," I write, "How is your son doing? Have you guys picked the destination for your next trip yet?" This simple personal gesture stands out and makes them more likely to respond and continue to build a relationship with me.

I came up with this networking idea on my own, and I follow through on it (and others) in an effort to stand out and be remembered. The effort has been minuscule in comparison to the results it has produced in my life. It has helped me ten times over not only with my goals but also in lessening the time it has taken me to achieve those goals. This is why networking gets its own chapter in this book. It has jump-started my career numerous times; perhaps I could even call them shortcuts, but all legit and all done in good faith, as I always keep myself open for what I might be able to do for them in return.

NFL Notoriety

One thing I've learned as an NFL player is that nobody will *ever* be more interested in me than they are right *now*, while I'm actually wearing an NFL jersey. Therefore, it's vital for me to network, build relationships, and open as many doors as I can before I retire. There's a *stark* difference between how I'm treated as a current player and how I'll be treated as a former player. I have to take advantage of this platform while I have it. My strategy is if I open doors and let people see what I can bring to the table *now*, then once I'm done playing those same doors will *stay* open.

Unfortunately, some professional athletes think they're too big time to network, to reach out to companies, or talk to people who are interested in working with them. They fall victim to the "Shut up and dribble mindset," which essentially means focusing on their sport and *nothing* else. They figure they'll network and find opportunities once they retire. What they don't understand is that they can leverage their playing years into a money-making retirement.

DEVON DEBUNKS

"It's not what you know, it's who you know."

 I'm sure you've heard that expression before, right? Well, it's wrong. To succeed in life, you need both—you need to pursue and utilize *what* you know and *who* you know. For example, if I wasn't putting in the work in football (the what I know) and networking/connecting with Master Joe Kim (the who I know), I wouldn't have improved my pass rushing to earn those fourteen sacks over two years while having two of my best years in the league. In real estate, it wasn't enough for me to see how many real estate investments worth investing in came across my desk. If I didn't put the work into learning about real estate so I could understand and identify good deals and also network with the right real estate experts who taught me so much, I wouldn't have the success I have had.

But Devon, I don't like mingling with people at events.

"If you want to go fast, go alone; but if you want to go far, go together."

I am a gregarious guy. I love talking to people at events. Maybe you're not an extrovert, and the idea of mingling and talking to people makes you want to hide in a corner. That's okay. If you commit to attending an event or meeting, you aren't required to talk to everyone. Just talk to *someone*. Talking to one person is better than talking to no one. Make one solid connection at a business marketing event or a party, get that person's business card, and write some notes on it to help you remember them.

Remember Their Name

It surprises me how often people don't take the time to remember someone's name when doing so can make such an impact. People are flattered when someone comes up to them and says their name while reintroducing themselves. That love of being recognized and hearing your name spoken is part of the human DNA. At the end of the day people want to feel valued. Something as simple as remembering their name can do that, so make the effort. They will probably think, "Wow, I only met this guy one time and he remembered my name already?" Now you have that person's attention, and they will always think highly of you. (One way to remember is to use alliteration, such as Awesome Andy or Gentle George.)

Every NFL team has a nutrition team that makes our meals, an equipment staff that gets our equipment ready and keeps our locker room clean, and a training room staff that keeps us healthy. I do the best I can to remember everyone's name in each department. I also make sure to address them by their name and have a conversation with them.

Write a Note

After you meet someone, write a handwritten note telling them how pleased you are to have met them and how you hope to connect again in the future. You can also write a note expressing your

At a networking event
Photo credit: Devon Kennard

appreciation for a job well done or thanking someone for what they said or did for you. That one token of appreciation can lead to opportunities down the road.

Next-Level Networking

Networking is only the first part of building relationships. Now it's time to do your due diligence. You've met someone at an event who intrigues you, but how do you know if they are someone with whom you really want to work? Can you trust them? Are they reliable? Are they diligent? Can they solve problems or do they crumble? Here are some questions you should ask yourself before taking a relationship to the next level:

Do they conduct business in a manner that is compatible with how I do business? If they do, I know it's somebody I want on my team. I can't work with someone if we do not see eye to eye on how business should be conducted. An example of this is someone who isn't punctual. I take it as a sign of disrespect if someone consistently shows up late or cancels scheduled meetings with me. So once I recognize that in someone, I steer clear of them to avoid future conflict.

Do they bring value to me? Do I bring value to them? What value does that person have from which you can benefit? Is it knowledge? Is it expertise? Is it their connections? Is it where they work? It could be an array of things, but figure out which it is that you are looking for. How will a relationship with this person help your business and move you closer to your goals? You don't have to remember every single detail about every person you meet. Just pick one or two things that stand out as memorable and/or relevant to you, keeping it simple yet focused. That will take you a long way.

In return, and this is very important, you must always be thinking about what you can provide to that person. I can guarantee that they are sizing you up the same way. I might meet someone and want access to some of the investments they have or their real estate connections. In return, they might want more capital for a business venture. So they have the deal and I have the capital. The best relationships come from finding things between you and the other person that are mutually beneficial. Don't just be thinking about yourself.

If the person brings value to you, but you can't bring value to them (or vice versa), it's still okay to work together. Down the road, there might be an opportunity to change that.

Is their behavior a deal breaker? Before you decide to build a relationship with someone, think about your *nonnegotiables*. My nonnegotiables are people who are detailed, professional, and respectful of my time. I don't need people who are careless, skip steps, take forever to respond to emails, texts, and calls, or who are unreliable or unprofessional in any way. It doesn't mean they are unable to or don't do great work, but that kind of behavior drives me nuts, and in such a case it's best that we do not work together.

. For example, my now former accountant failed to tell me, until a week before it was due, that there was a huge tax payment that I needed to make. If he had been on top of details and deadlines, I should have been given plenty of notice. As a result of this huge financial error, I fired him and found a new firm with which to work. By mid-November that year, the new firm had already given me an estimate of what I was going to pay in taxes for that year—and it wouldn't even be due until April the following year. They also gave me a report with steps I could take to reduce my tax burden. The new firm costs more money than the accountant, but they were so prompt that they put me in a position to pay significantly less in taxes. They have been worth every penny of their fee. Now I'm able to plan ahead. What are *your* nonnegotiables?

Are they a team player? My team works together. My accountant needs to be able to communicate with my financial adviser and with my agent. Everybody has to be kept abreast of what I'm doing and be able to interact with each other. It's really important to me that my team is all on the same side with no conflicts with one another.

Do they handle tough times? You might not be able to find out how someone handles tough times until you are knee deep in a crisis, but keep your eyes open and ears tuned. How does the other person handle the difficulties? Are they a confident problem solver or do they get stressed and make careless mistakes? Maybe someone else you know worked with them. Listen, but keep in mind there are two sides to every bad story. Not everything is going to go smoothly all the time, but pay close attention when something does go wrong. Because of the pandemic, I really got to see how the people I am working with handle tough times, and, for the most part, they handled them really well. I'm proud of the people with whom I've surrounded myself. They didn't always make the right decisions, but they communicated well and found the best solutions that moved us forward.

Negative Networking

Here's an example of painting yourself into a corner. What if you've networked with someone you don't want to work with, but you feel an obligation to follow up because you took their business card. Don't sweat it or fret it: casual connections will probably weed themselves out over time. It's okay to keep things open-ended by looking at the upside: even if an individual is someone who does not interest you now, they might be a good connection later. Don't burn bridges, even in your head.

If I *really* can't picture myself working with someone for a lifetime, then I don't work with them for a day. That being said, I'm not looking for a bunch of Devon clones. My nonnegotiables are important. So is whether or not they are good at what they do. There are certain standards of business that I regard as necessary to build relationships. If I waver from that, it's like building a house with straw.

My Team

So who is on my team? It is a combination of people whose services I pay for and people whose friendship I trust and whose relationships are mutually beneficial. Your team members will look different compared to mine, but my roster includes my financial adviser, a property manager, my wife, financial lenders, my marketing team, my agent, trainers, real estate mentors, my accountant, and my spiritual mentor.

Find a Financial Adviser

To find a financial adviser, ask friends and family for trusted recommendations. There are many different types of financial advisers, so you need to find one who fits your individual needs and budget. Visit the National Association of Personal Financial Advisors website, https://www.napfa.org/, for tips and resources.

It's important to note that not everybody that is in your network is on your team. For example, I once sent out a tweet about an investment and woke up the next morning to more than a hundred direct messages from other athletes and professionals asking me how they can get involved and wanting to invest with me. These people became potential team members, but I didn't need them right then. I was focusing on my own portfolio, but I knew I would foster some of those relationships in the future. Your team might come from your network, but don't confuse your network with your team.

So who would make a great member of your team?

I was once asked if I feel like I'm always "on" everywhere I go since networking is important to me. For the most part, maybe I am, but it's not strategic. I firmly believe that you never know where any relationship can go, so meeting people has just become a part of who I am.

One of my favorite things to do is go out and have a nice meal and a few glasses of wine (this is definitely different from my younger self that loved to hang out at bars and clubs all night long). In Arizona, when I go to my favorite restaurants, I make it a point to talk to the managers and, no surprise, get their business cards. If you ever visit Scottsdale, Arizona, and think you'll be getting a last-minute reservation at one of the trendy restaurants, forget it. During busy seasons, restaurants such as Steak 44, Mastro's, Toca Madera, and Maple & Ash are booked out weeks in advance. Thanks to my relationships, if I need to conduct a business meeting or if someone comes to town and I'd like to take them out to enjoy themselves, I can reach out for a reservation because of my networking.

Social Media Networking

Today, many people network through social media. There are Facebook groups and Twitter communities for pretty much any interest. Join them and start talking to others who have the same interests that you do. You can also DM people through platforms such as Instagram and LinkedIn. I try to interact and respond to those who DM me, which can lead to opportunities. I've been a guest on multiple podcasts from having met people through social media. For example, through Instagram, I met soccer player Amobi

Okugo, who founded *A Frugal Athlete Podcast Network*, a show I thoroughly enjoy. I reached out to him, and he asked me to come on the podcast.

Here's another example of how networking through social media can pay off. For my "Reading with DK" book club, I once chose *Rich Dad Poor Dad* by Robert Kiyosaki as our book of the month and posted it on my Instagram. One of Kiyosaki's managers saw the post and *they* reached out to *me*. As a result, I appeared on Robert Kiyosaki's podcast, *The Rich Dad Radio Show*, and YouTube channel, The Rich Dad Channel. That was a really cool full-circle moment for me to be talking to Kiyosaki, someone who really changed my life. I also appeared on PBS's *The Great American Read* after posting that *To Kill a Mockingbird* was one of my favorite books. This just goes to show you that media and brands are using social media to find partnerships. Leverage this as much as you can.

I haven't stopped networking since my days at USC, and I hope I never will. My needs have changed as I have gotten older and as I have embarked on new ventures. I'm always going to need new team members and always want to build out my network. If you want to continue to be successful in the future, you'll always network and build relationships.

Be intentional about everyone who is in your circle of influence. A network is a living thing that is steadily changing and evolving, so it's important that you are always assessing it and the team you have around you. The right team can help make you or help break you!

CHAPTER TEN

You've Got Mail(box) Money!

I like when money makes a difference,
but money doesn't make you different.
—Drake

Imagine waking up in the morning and having more money in your bank account than you did the day before. That's because during the night, a tenant in one of your properties made a rent payment, or a syndication you are in sent you a dividend payment. While you were dreaming of your next vacation, you got paid. How awesome is that!

Most people want to live life on their terms, whether it's working only ten hours a week or working a nine-to-five job that they love—the problem is their salary might not cover their bills or give them extra play-around or retirement money. Mailbox money (a reminder that it's also called passive income) is the key to unlocking financial freedom because it's as easy as making money while you sleep. In fact, that is exactly what is happening. What a concept!

As I mentioned earlier, it's called mailbox money because, once upon a time, people would go to their mailboxes to find a load of checks. While paper checks are sometimes still sent out, most of the mailbox money people earn is directly deposited into their bank accounts nowadays, but the concept of earning while you do (almost) nothing remains the same.

Now, mailbox money is a huge part of my financial portfolio. I earn money from multiple income streams, including my real estate properties and syndication investments, as well as royalties from this book and other projects.

My first financial goal in the NFL was to make enough money to provide a foundation for my family. Mission accomplished. Next, I wanted to establish enough mailbox money that I would continue to live my life—my version of the American dream—the way I see it even after the checks from the NFL dry up. When I finally retire from pro football, I want my best years to be ahead of me, not behind me.

Thanks to these income streams, I'm confident my family and I will be able to live the life that I want us to live and do what we want to do, even after my NFL career is over. I still have a mortgage to pay, two children to take care of as well as another seventy years (hopefully) to live with my wife. Whether you make a healthy salary or not, mailbox money should be something you aspire to have.

DK Spends Crazy Money Now!

Remember Devon the teen who wouldn't loan money to anyone or Devon the NFL rookie who shipped an old car to New York because he didn't want to buy a new one until he knew his football career was moving forward? Times have changed. Let's be clear though; I am still very conservative when it comes to spending and investing money, but my financial situation looks different than it used to. I'm earning enough to enjoy a little more of the finer things I've always wanted, but I use my mailbox money for those purchases, and I'm not spending crazy money in proportion to where I am financially.

Some financial gurus have been spouting unrealistic advice. They say that to achieve your financial goals you should live off a specified amount of money. Then, even as you begin to make more, you should continue to live off of that same amount. I remember telling myself I, too, would do that, but I learned that it's completely impractical. For example, in college, after all of my bills were paid, I lived off of $300 a month. When I got into the NFL I estimated that I would live off of $1,000 a month (after all my bills were paid) and feel like I'm balling in comparison to college. In truth, once I got signed, I found it extremely challenging to consistently spend less than $1,000 a month. Something *always* came up. I was playing in New York, so airfare home to Arizona cost me $300 to $400 each time I visited. A dinner in New York City could easily cost $200. If a new pair of Jordans came out, there's another $150. I had trainers to pay, Uber and Lyft rides, and so on. In comparison to many of my teammates, I was extremely frugal, but when you compare it to the original budget that I set for myself, I was regularly over.

Hear me out for a second. When you get a raise, start a new side hustle, or have a good amount of mailbox money coming in, your first move should not be to start spending it; on that part I am in sync with the financial gurus. At some point, though, your earnings will increase, and you will likely start to spend more. That's when you will need to adjust your budget.

Let's say that you currently live off a $50,000 per year salary. You worked hard to become debt-free. Now, you have extra income to play with and use to invest or build more income streams. Your income grows but you are still living off of $50,000 per year for another year or two. I'm willing to bet that eventually you will grow comfortable with your new financial situation. Then you decide you want to enjoy more of what you have earned and saved, so you will likely begin to spend more than your budget. Even if you are very conservative, you might find yourself, at the very least, going to a steakhouse and ordering the high-end Wagyu steak instead of the NY strip.

This has happened several times to me in my career. I'll give you two examples. First, when I was in college, on the rare occasion I did go out, I *hated* riding with my friends. Typically, whoever I hung out with would want to stay later than I wanted to and I would feel stuck. I could not afford to pay for a ride home, so I would be required to wait until my friends were ready to go. Once I joined the NFL, I would without hesitation ride into the city to socialize with some of my teammates, because I knew I could afford to catch an Uber home whenever I wanted to without giving a second thought to how much I was spending. Now, a $50 Uber home every now and then was not going to have much, if any, negative impact on me; it wasn't going to drain any of my accounts. This goes to show that once you start to make a little money, your willingness to spend money on certain things can change as well. Nobody talks about this, *especially* those financial gurus.

For me, this "spending creep," as I call it, affects my travel. I used to always get the cheapest flight. It didn't matter if that meant that I needed to take a red-eye or sit in the cramped middle seat.

That changed once I reached my sixth year in the NFL, when I hit a good enough financial position that I could treat myself to a first-class seat or pay extra for an exit row seat with more legroom. I am a fairly big guy, and I will no longer squish into the middle seat on a flight!

My advice? Keep the spending creep within reason. If you get to the point where you are bringing in a good amount of mailbox money each month (and only you can judge what that amount is) buying the high-end Wagyu instead of the NY strip occasionally is okay. But spend within reason. Don't be the person who generates consistent mailbox money each month and then finds a way to spend it all every month, too.

DEVON DEBUNKS

 How often do you hear people say that mailbox money is doing something *once* and sitting back to reap the rewards? That's not completely true, so let's debunk this myth. With my real estate investments, I earn mailbox money every month, but I still have to travel to the properties a few times a year at least, work with the property management team, and make sure the buildings are in good condition and everything is okay with the tenants. After I purchase the property, my hands-on work is minimal and can be handled with a couple of hours of work a month max, but I still have to do *something*.

If you are someone who develops a course online to teach others what you do, there is work you need to do before your launch. Once you've created the course, it could definitely become a mailbox money generator for you, but you will likely still need to market it so people sign up, manage and keep the site up to date, oversee the payment systems, and so on. Hopefully, this maintenance won't take a ton of time, but it is still work. Are you cut out for it?

The same goes with writing a book. You want to sell copies years from now, so you will need to promote it and maybe even update the information to keep it relevant, maybe even issue actual revisions of the book as warranted from time to time (as long as it is still selling and therefore you are not chasing "bad money"—or no money—with good money).

For example, I sit down with David, my financial adviser, four times a year to review how each real estate syndication is performing and to double-check the books to make sure I have been paid out appropriately. It takes us about eight hours a year in total but it's pivotal in making sure we are holding the GPs (general partners) accountable and I'm being a good steward of my finances and investments.

Other Types of Mailbox Money

It's important to note that *any* business, investment, or idea can become a mailbox money generator for you. What business can you start? What investment can you invest in? What service can you provide? Here are a few ideas:

Invest in real estate: Hopefully, by now we've established that investing in real estate (properties in really any asset class, but here's a few to consider: single-family homes, Airbnbs, multifamily, and commercial) is a fantastic way to earn mailbox money. Later, I will break down how it works for me.

Buy a vending machine: Believe it or not, there are people who make a ton of mailbox money by buying a vending machine and placing it in a prime location (school, office building, park). Once you do that, all you have to do is refill the vending machine and take the cash out. That's mailbox money!

Create an online course: Do you know how to quilt? Fix cars? Paint? Cook? Can you create videos or write ebooks that teach others how to do what you do? Whatever your expertise is, there are people who would pay to learn how to do it, too. Take the time to create a detailed course around a skill set you have and sell it. You put in the majority of the effort up front and just have to manage, update, and market it once you have it going.

DEVON DEBUNKS

 Many people think that the stock market is a great way to earn mailbox money; I've invested in it, too. Yes, you invest and when your stock appreciates, you earn money. History has shown that when you invest in the stock market over a period of ten-plus years, you will reap the benefits of a portfolio that grows 8–12 percent. I'm not here to argue that, but bear in mind that perceived appreciation is not realized unless you sell your stock. Depending on how it's structured, it can be profitable. Overall, though, I do not think the stock market is the *best* mailbox money strategy. What if all of your money was tied up in the stock market and you suddenly lost your job or had another financial emergency? It's not easy to get your hands on your money without jumping a few hurdles like the IRS.

You could sell shares of your stock, of course, but now you've weakened your ownership and stock position. In my opinion, having other means of more accessible—or liquid—mailbox money is really the key to financial peace of mind. This is why I think of the stock market more as a long-term appreciation play.

Affiliate income: As I mentioned earlier, affiliate programs are a great way to earn mailbox money if you're a podcaster or own a website or blog.

Any business: As long as you structure the business in a way that you can own all or part of it, and it can operate without you physically being there or working regularly, it can be a mailbox money generator. I've seen people do this with training facilities, restaurants, franchising businesses, and so on. So what business can you start?

DK's BIG Mailbox Money Markers:

- **Minimum goal:** generate mailbox money of $1,000 every month.
- **Midgoal:** Generate enough mailbox money to cover your major expenses.
- **Big goal:** Generate enough mailbox money to cover your entire lifestyle.
- **Dream goal:** Make so much mailbox money that your ideal lifestyle is covered, you're saving money, and you have extra to reinvest or spend how you please.

Inspiration

LeBron James is one of my idols. What he has achieved both on and off the basketball court is remarkable. Yes, he's a multimillionaire—earning more than $380 million in the NBA, but he's doubled that—and then some—*off* the court. He has invested in businesses that provide him with major mailbox money, such as Blaze Pizza and Lobos 1707 tequila, a Black woman–led company. Then he became an extraordinary media mogul. He formed SpringHill Company, which is worth more than $300 million today. I do not know what LeBron's day-to-day looks like, but I am willing to bet he puts most of his focus on his basketball career and all of his other endeavors are mailbox money generators for him.

I've also looked up to Magic Johnson and his business acumen, including his investments in Starbucks, the Los Angeles Sparks of the WNBA, the Los Angeles Dodgers (he has since sold off his partnership), and Major League Soccer's Los Angeles Football Club. In an interview, Johnson once said, "The magic secret sauce is really hiring the right people." What I took from that quote was that Magic does not want or have the time or skill set to run all of his business ventures. He needs to hire the right people so that he can focus on the things he wants to while still generating mailbox money from these other ventures. Shaquille O'Neal has invested in Papa John's, Five Guys, and various fitness centers. He's another guy who played in the NBA for a long time and now is a sports broadcaster. His day-to-day is not running Papa John's or Five Guys, so what does that tell us? Those are mailbox money generators for him!

Dwayne "The Rock" Johnson played college football and aimed for an NFL career, but he didn't get drafted. A few years later, with only seven dollars left in his pocket, he shifted his life's path and followed in the footsteps of his professional wrestler father. He went on to WWE superstardom and then became the richest actor in Hollywood. As of 2022, he is worth $320 million—from $7 to $320 million—and he hasn't stopped there. Honestly, he doesn't have to work anymore. He works because he wants to work. He also added new business ventures to his repertoire, including Teremana, a tequila company, ownership of the XFL, and Zoa Energy. Talk about mailbox money. He has leveraged his brand and stardom into multiple businesses that are all generating mailbox money. That's big time.

Before his untimely passing, Nipsey Hussle, one of my favorite rappers I told you about earlier, released a hundred copies of his album *Mailbox Money* and charged $1,000 per copy. He was then asked, in an interview by *Complex*, about an article he tweeted about passive income. Here is what he responded, "Hip-hop is inspired by the hustler. It's hip-hop to do it this way. The model is switching. What's your bragging right? You're going platinum? That used to be the metric of success. But to me, it's like what do you own? What's your position? Can you make shit move? Do you have power? Do you have control of your destiny? Do you have to jump through hoops? Do you have to play games and appeal to people whose interest isn't about making quality products? This is how a real hustler hustles."

I agree with Hussle, but I do not think what he said applies only to rappers. I think it is time we *all* start thinking this way. You do not have to be LeBron, Magic, Shaq, or The Rock to flip the bag—double your income and create mailbox money. Ultimately, I truly believe that generating mailbox money is a pivotal key to whatever your American dream looks like. So what are you going to do to start generating it?

It's a blessing that my career has gone the way it has, but it has also awarded time to push me toward newer and bigger goals, including real estate investments, keynote speaking, and becoming an author. Like I said in chapter 1, "Football is what I do. It's not who I am." And now I have become so much more, and you can, too.

Mailbox money is the key to living life on *your* terms and doing what you want, when you want, how you want, and with whom you want. The more mailbox money you generate, the more you can focus on the things *you* care about and want to do, which means you're living *your* American dream!

CHAPTER ELEVEN

Get Comfortable Being Uncomfortable

Wherever your treasure is,
there the desires of your heart will also be.
—Matthew 6:21

I loved my time playing for the Detroit Lions. I met some great friends there—Christian Jones, Darius Slay, Quandre Diggs, Marvin Jones, Romeo Okwara, and Matthew Stafford, just to name a few. To be named team captain among such a great group of guys, combined with the on-field success I had in Detroit, made those years some of my favorites from my entire career thus far.

In the Bible, Jesus states that those who hear His words and do them are wise builders. These are the people who have built their homes on rock-solid foundations. The winds howl, the rains come—even a flood arrives—but the house still stands firm. Jesus also states that those who hear His words but fail to live by them are foolish builders.

I was fortunate that at this point I was a wise builder. I had built a rock-solid foundation in my life—trusting God's plan for my life, having a good support system that consisted of family and friends, and being content in knowing I did everything I could to become extraordinary in my own life. But it was in Detroit where my heart was broken by the harsh brutality of the NFL. It was this foundation that I would lean on to get me through the biggest blindside in my career.

It was January 2020, and I was one month away from marrying Camille, the love of my life, on a leap-year day, February 29. A few weeks before the wedding, we were at the Super Bowl at Hard Rock Stadium in Miami Gardens, Florida, for the Walter Payton Man of the Year Award ceremony. I had been selected as a finalist, and accompanying me to the ceremony were Detroit Lions president Ron Wood, GM Bob Quinn, head coach Matt Patricia, and their respective families. We were all sitting at the same table, talking, laughing, and having a great time.

I was proud of the work I had done to get me to this moment, and I had been nominated with a group of great NFL players, including Brandon Carr, Cam Newton, Jarvis Landry, Calais Campbell, Richard Sherman, and others. The winner of this prestigious award receives $250,000 donated to the winner's charity of choice. All other nominees receive up to $40,000 donated to their charity of choice.

One of the coolest things about being a Walter Payton Man of the Year finalist was the experience in Miami during Super Bowl week. I rubbed shoulders with some of the most respected former and current NFL players. I kept telling Camille that I was in football heaven. We attended the NFL Honors event and then, on the bus headed to the Super Bowl, I was with Hall of Famers (HOFers), eating lunch with premier All-Pro players, and being considered for one of if not *the* most prestigious awards the NFL has to offer! The entire experience was definitely a *you made it* moment for me.

With my wife, Camille, at the 2020 NFL Honors in Miami
Photo credit: Rich Graessle/PPI/Icon Sportswire via Getty Images

Calais Campbell took the award that year, but it was still nice to be nominated as a finalist. I used the $40,000 I received to sponsor the Devon Kennard Scholarship Fund, where I gave scholarships to deserving kids who were a part of the Midnight Golf Program (I talk more about this charity in chapter 14).

Post-Wedding Mayhem

Fast-forward to the morning of my wedding day when Coach Patricia called to congratulate me.

"Devon, you're such a big part of what we're doing here in Detroit," he told me. "We love you and are excited for your big day today. Congratulations."

My heart was full. I thanked Coach Patricia for calling me and was excited to start our special day. The Lions QB, Matthew Stafford, and about fifteen other teammates came to our wedding. The night was a blur and the most turnt wedding that I have ever been to—and I'm not being biased!

At this moment in time, everything in my life was going great, both personally and professionally. When some of my closest friends from high school came to visit me in Detroit, they couldn't believe how much the city had embraced me. After all, I was still just their boy from Ahwatukee, Arizona, but here in Detroit my face was on billboards, on the side of the stadium, and on the tickets to get into the stadium. Mikey Flemister, my best friend since kindergarten, even said, "Man, you are really *that* dude now, ha ha!"

I was on cloud nine.

A few weeks after my wedding, mid-March, was the start of the NFL free agency period. Immediately, the Lions signed inside linebacker Jamie Collins to a three-year, multimillion-dollar contract. I was an outside linebacker and one of their best defensive players at the time. I had outperformed my contract, things were going well, and my agent and I were already in the Lions' ear about a contract extension or renegotiation, so I didn't think this move would affect me. Two days into free agency Lions GM Bob Quinn called and said point-blank: "Hey, Devon, we just signed Jamie

Collins and we can't afford to give you what you want, so we're just going to have to let you go."

I was stunned. I was heartbroken. I had felt loved here and now I felt discarded, all because the third year of my contract was not guaranteed, and the team could just get rid of me.

The situation with Detroit hurt more than what happened in New York. In New York, I had outperformed my contract, but I knew that there was a new GM and coaching staff coming into the Giants' organization, so I had already planned on testing free agency and taking the best offer presented to me. So when the Giants did not offer anything competitive, I was sad to be leaving but was ready for that reality. What also differed is that the Giants never cut me. I played out my entire contract and was a free agent. I was just hoping that they would offer me enough so I could stay.

My agent, Erik, told them that he couldn't believe the team was doing this to me. To add more insult to injury, the Lions were actually going to try to trade me to the Pittsburgh Steelers instead of releasing me. That's not what I wanted. Pittsburgh already had two great outside linebackers in Bud Dupree and T. J. Watt. I felt like I was at the top of my game and wanted to go somewhere where I had an opportunity to take the next step in my career, but honestly, it was what it was. I asked them to release me so I could become a free agent. I was coming off two really good seasons in Detroit, so I knew that I would get an opportunity to play somewhere.

We went back and forth on this for a while, and ultimately they agreed to release me instead of trading me.

The Grand Canyon State

Erik, my agent, who represented coaches and players for the Arizona Cardinals, happened to know that they were looking for an outside linebacker. The Cardinals were surprised to see that the Lions released me and showed immediate interest.

In a matter of days, I had a new, three-year contract with the Cardinals. As stunned as I was over what had happened with the Lions, it never once crossed my mind that something wouldn't happen for me. But I still couldn't believe how my time in Detroit ended. I had a home in Detroit that my wife and I and our first-born, Camryn, realized we would never be going back to. Hiring a moving company to pack up our things and drive them to Arizona was surreal.

I also felt like I never got the closure I wanted in Detroit. I never had the opportunity to say goodbye to any of the amazing people I met during my time there. The last time I saw them I had said, "See you later," not "Goodbye."

There are moments in life you feel you don't deserve. This was one of them. You will think that, whatever it is that happened, it isn't right or fair, but these moments show you how important it is to be grounded in who you are and what you believe in. Do not let that waver for anyone or anything. Without that rock-solid foundation, you will be absolutely crushed when unexpected things happen.

To help get me through all of my own feelings about what had happened in Detroit, I leaned into my faith and prayed. I feel like my relationship with God has been the bedrock for my life in times of uncertainty, knowing that God must have a different plan for me. But it was the NFL, where it's essential to have a short memory to handle things like what happened to me. I was going to miss

Detroit, but it was time to make lemonade out of lemons. I signed a contract with the Cardinals for $20 million with $12.25 million guaranteed. It was time to move on, especially when I had this great opportunity in Arizona. That's when I realized, "God knows what He is doing!"

Signing with the Cardinals was really a dream come true for me. They practiced fifteen minutes away from where I grew up. In an interesting twist of events, Camille and I had decided to purchase our long-term home in Arizona while I was still with the Lions. Arizona was home to us and where we wanted to raise our children and live in the off-season. But despite my growing assets and portfolio, the bank found out about my release from the Lions and said they would not let me close on our property while I was unemployed. They would not let us purchase our dream home until I could prove my employment from the Cardinals.

It's hard to believe that this almost cost us our home, but it taught me a valuable lesson about banks—they do *not* care about how much money or what kind of investments you have. Above anything else, the most important factor in approving a loan is the security of knowing that you are employed and making a high enough salary that you can afford the home you are purchasing.

(Side note: this also taught me to find other lending options that would work for my situation when I became self-employed after leaving the NFL. I am not planning on getting another job working for someone else. I will run my own businesses and invest in real estate, but without that W-2, lenders and banks are going to make loan approval tough for me.)

Later, we did buy the home, and I then turned my attention to my new team. I had already convinced myself that they were bringing me in to be their guy, so let's do this!

It did not help things, though, when I went into training camp with a strained left calf and wasn't feeling 100 percent. I was extremely frustrated with the injury, but I pushed through. I felt good enough to practice but not good enough to be at the top of my game. I am not the kind of guy to make excuses, and I wanted to impress my new teammates and coaches, so I did what I've done many times before—I put in even more time with the trainers and strength staff to get my body to feel stronger.

In just the first three games of the year, I had six tackles, two sacks, and a few TFLs (tackles-for-loss). It was a solid start, but at the end of the third game against my former team, the Detroit Lions, I strained my *right* calf. It cost me two games—against the Carolina Panthers and the New York Jets. I came back, but probably too soon. The next two games, versus the Dallas Cowboys and Seattle Seahawks, were probably two of my worst games since I started in the NFL. It's not that I played really bad, but if you watch the film, you could just tell my calf was bothering me and I was not playing up to my capabilities.

And then I caught COVID-19.

At the time I tested positive, it was required by the NFL that I remain out of action for at least a week. During that week, the Cardinals traded for Markus Golden, a good friend of mine who happens to play the same position that I do. For the rest of the 2020 season, my playing time was minimal at best. When I did get onto the field, I was effective, but I didn't get any opportunities to rush the passer. I ended the season with nineteen tackles and three sacks. The Cardinals kept me for the 2021 season—not that they had much choice. Erik and I negotiated a contract where I was guaranteed $6.2 million in year two of my deal no matter what, so why not keep me around? The Cardinals used me in a similar role in

2021 as they did at the end of 2020, and I ended the season playing in thirteen games and having twenty-four tackles.

When the 2021 season ended, my contract with Arizona was restructured. Here's how this went down: The Cardinals owed me $6.9 million for the 2022 season, but none of that was guaranteed. The Cardinals were planning to cut me unless we could come to terms on a deal for less money, and since I was still on the team and not an official free agent yet, I could not negotiate with any other team.

I wanted to stay in Arizona. I am very risk averse, so considering how the last few years with the Cardinals had gone, it was unclear how good of a deal I could get in free agency. My mindset was that if I can reach fair terms with the Cardinals and renegotiate my contract instead of getting cut or becoming a free agent, that is what I would do. Negotiations between Erik and the Cardinals GM Steve Keim got pretty heated because (1) Erik and I felt that I should make more money than what I signed for and (2) if I was going to sign for less, we at least wanted the contract guaranteed.

You would think I had learned from my ending experience with the Lions, but I allowed myself to get comfortable. When I signed with the Cardinals, I had thought everything was all good again. But I didn't have the same success on the field for the Cardinals as I did for the Lions. Going from being "the guy," a featured guy on a team, to "a guy," a role player, in a matter of one season, was a scenario I *never* saw coming. Honestly, I still struggle when I think about this. I'm playing in my hometown and for a team my father also played for! I had a different vision of how things would play out in Arizona.

When it comes to money, logic says that my peak earning potential is definitely behind me, and I'm okay with that. It's been nine years since I joined the NFL, and it's gone by very quickly. I believe I have a lot more football left in me, and my goal is to play a few more years, but I am taking it one year at a time. As I write this I have some doubt about what is in store for my NFL future, but anxiety is not part of the equation. Whether I never play another season in the NFL or I'm blessed to play another three to five years, I can confidently say I am financially ready for whatever happens next.

It turns out the Cardinals and I came to an agreement for less than I originally wanted, but they conceded on incentives to my contract that would allow me to make up to $2 million. No matter what my résumé suggests about my true worth, NFL teams will leverage their position to pay the least amount of money they can. That's the business of professional football.

These experiences of being unexpectedly released or traded are humbling, to say the least. First, I signed with the Giants, and they decided not to re-sign me. Then, I signed with Detroit and thought *I'm the man*, then I got cut. I signed with Arizona, my playtime is reduced, and I'm contemplating my future.

It's taken time, but I ultimately found comfort in being uncomfortable. The good news though is I'm happy that I got to stay in Arizona, my home, and secure my ninth year in the NFL.

My journey has shown me that *nothing* is guaranteed in the NFL; you can never relax. When you do rest on your laurels, that's when the unexpected happens. I learned that the hard way in Detroit. Based on everything good that I did during my time in Detroit—on and off the field—I thought my job was "secure." In the end, I learned that no matter what team I am on or at what stage of my career I am at, that team is always looking to replace me.

So it was up to me to change things. I had to control the controllable. For me, I can control being the best possible version of myself I can be. If I'm always doing that, I am confident that I'm enough, but if/when the day comes when my best is not enough, I will still be at peace knowing I gave it my all. Are you at that point in your life? Whether or not you are, I'm passing along what I've learned through life to help you with yours.

Connect

Sharing this story about my stunning departure from the Lions and how it affected me emotionally was hard to do, but I wanted to tell it anyway. I believe this part of my story might connect with you, especially if you have faced unforeseen circumstances in your life or career, such as if you have been laid off, given a pay cut, or experienced an unwanted, perhaps undeserved, shift in responsibilities that you just didn't expect. Just remember, you can allow your circumstances to make you bitter or you can allow them to make you better.... I hope you choose the latter!

While all of this changing teams stuff has been happening with me, let's remember that off the gridiron I'm still building my own real estate empire. There is no give up in me, just more giddy-up. Let me walk you through some more about what I have done and still want to do, and how you can apply it to your circumstances and goals. After all, what is guaranteed in all of this? It's a fact that these NFL experiences of mine have made me even more dedicated to my financial goals. Why? Because I knew way back on draft day that one day it would be time to leave the game. My exit strategy has long been at work, practically dating back to when I walked under the virtual door marked Entrance into the NFL. I have worked hard to make sure I put myself in the best financial position I could be in when that time comes. Once you get comfortable being uncomfortable, you start making the right changes for you.

 Adaptability and handling change are key traits to flipping the bag. Life is unpredictable at times, and you will get punched in the mouth at some point, but how you pivot and respond is what matters most!

CHAPTER TWELVE

Real Estate Can Be for Everyone

Ninety percent of millionaires
became so through owning real estate.
—Andrew Carnegie

Andrew Carnegie was right. You *can* become wealthy by owning a home, but Carnegie wasn't talking about becoming rich by buying a home that you will live in and nothing else. The 90 percent of millionaires that he was talking about made their money by investing in a property that someone else lives in while the millionaire reaps the financial rewards.

But what about everything you've heard about the benefits of owning your own home? Do these comments sound familiar?

"Buy a home. It's part of the American dream."

"Buy a home. You'll get a lot of tax breaks."

"Buy a home. When you sell it, you'll make a lot of money."

Yes, owning your dream home is an awesome accomplishment, and it does come with many financial benefits. It can increase your net worth over time and provide you with equity that you can use for renovations on your property or to use as the down payment on your next property. But the problem with doing a cash-out refinance on the home you live in and taking out the equity is that your monthly payment will likely increase. Unfortunately, many people cannot afford a higher mortgage payment. Therefore, many Americans have built-in equity from the home they live in that they cannot really tap into. With all of this in mind, when I was looking to make money in real estate that would help get me closer to my financial goals, I bought an investment property instead of my own home and kept renting my East Coast apartment.

Why did I do that? Because I now owned a property that someone else was paying the mortgage on through rental payments. As years passed my property appreciated, but rent also increased, so over time I could in fact do a cash-out refinance, draw money from this investment property, invest it into the down payment of another property, and still have rental income that covers the mortgage. This is distinctly different than doing this in a property where you have to pay the mortgage yourself.

LOC is A-Okay

There actually is another way that a home can be an asset while you are still living in it. After living in the home for a few years, you begin to build up equity. Take a line of credit from that equity (HELOC) and use it to buy other real estate or investments. For example, I have a friend who paid $1.5M for his home, all in cash. Honestly, that is a lot of money to put into a property that you are living in versus investing in. His logic was sound, though: a mortgage is most people's largest expense, so by paying cash he eliminated that expense, which helps keep his monthly spending down significantly. When he finds another real estate investment he is interested in and needs capital, he will use a line of credit on his home equity at a low-interest rate and use that money for his real estate investment.

How does it benefit him financially? Let's look at some what-if numbers. Suppose his HELOC interest rate is 5 percent and he uses that loan money to invest in a syndication or to buy a property that will give him a dividend of 10 percent. He will thus earn the difference of 5 percent, which goes right back to him.

If he sells that investment property at a profit, he can use those funds to pay off the HELOC he took on his own home. Then, the next investment deal comes around and he does the same thing, again and again.

It's important to note that you do not need to buy your home fully in cash, like my friend did, in order to do the same thing. You can tap into the equity of your home even if you didn't buy your entire home in cash.

Earlier in the book we briefly discussed assets and liabilities. When you buy a home to live in, it definitely is an asset, but please do not forget that you have to provide a down payment, pay property taxes every year and a mortgage every month, and pay all the utility bills and any maintenance that comes with the property. Based on this, the home you live in has characteristics of a liability that must be acknowledged.

Your home does not truly make you money until you sell it. How much money will your property actually make while you own it? You need to run the numbers in order to figure this out, and it's something I do before I even put an offer down on a home. First, estimate the amount of the down payment you will need (it's usually somewhere between 3 percent and 25 percent of the cost of the property) and your living expenses on that property for a year, including mortgage payments, property taxes, and utility bills. Once you have that estimate, multiply that number by how many years you plan to live in that home. That total will give you a rough idea of what it will cost to live there for that period of time. Then you can calculate how much you will need to sell it for one day to turn your property into a true asset.

For example, let's say that you want to buy a home that's on the market for $500,000 and you have 10 percent for a down payment of $50,000. You plan to live in the house for five years and then sell it. You have estimated that the down payment, plus the mortgage payments, property taxes, and utility bills over five years total about $150,000. For that new home to be an asset, you need to pocket more than $150,000 in profit at the time of the sale. If you pocket less than $150,000, you did not make money on that property and it did not serve its purpose as an asset. (Keep in mind this

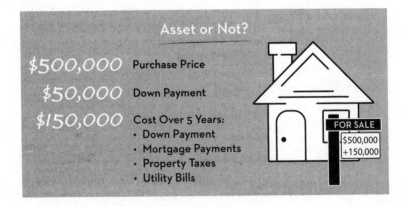

Asset or Not?

$500,000 Purchase Price

$50,000 Down Payment

$150,000 Cost Over 5 Years:
• Down Payment
• Mortgage Payments
• Property Taxes
• Utility Bills

FOR SALE
$500,000
+150,000

is a simplified example. Some real estate investors will say that it still served as an asset because there were tax benefits in owning the property over that time period, too, so it was still a good deal.)

Now, of course, it's okay to live in your home forever. You might also want to pass it down to your children. It's also okay if you buy a home and sell it five years later, only to break even or make just a small profit because of changes in either your life or in the real estate market. That home still provided you and your family with shelter, and for that, it was worth the money. I just want you to know and understand the numbers before you buy a home so you know how you can leverage your assets. Again, nobody teaches us this in school. We're just told that the American dream is home-ownership, but how can you make sure the home you buy and live in serves you not just as shelter but also financially?

Taking it a step further, what if you were taught to take your same down payment and buy a $500,000 duplex. You live in one of the units and rent out the other. The rent you charge your tenant covers your monthly mortgage payment and should give you a little extra mailbox money, so you are essentially living in your home for free. Now let's say that over the course of the years that you live there, the value of that duplex increases. At this point, all of the expenses have been paid for with the rental income from the tenant, so the only money you have invested is your initial $50,000 down payment. Now, when you sell the duplex if you profit more than $50,000, that investment was truly a revenue-generating and appreciating asset.

Or let's say that you don't sell the property, you just refinance it since it's appreciated so much in the five years you have lived there. You decide to refinance your mortgage at a lower interest rate. You are able to pull $70,000 of equity out of the property, which is the original $50,000 you invested plus an extra $20,000. You still own the property with no money in the deal. Now you can take that $70,000 and buy another place for you to live and rent your current home to another tenant. You've just increased your mailbox money and, most likely, the double rent from the duplex will cover some of your mortgage in your new place as well. I'll say it again— nobody teaches us this in school.

When you invest in a rental property, it immediately starts generating regular mailbox money as well as tax deductions for owning and operating that home. And, of course, if you sell the property after it has appreciated, you will make a profit.

Yes, there is work involved when you own a rental property. You need to keep that home in good condition for the tenant, and the more rental properties you add to your portfolio, the more work you have to do and the more tenants you have to deal with. But, to me, the benefits outweigh all the work you need to do, especially when you can hire property management to handle most of the legwork.

Before we deep dive into the rest of my real estate investing success and how you can achieve it, too, know that my journey is only one of many, *many* different directions available to you out there. I invested in single-family properties and duplexes as well as syndications, but you can flip homes, invest in short-term rentals, buy commercial real estate, invest in Airbnbs or other vacation rentals, or purchase multifamily units. You can even do a combination of any of them. All you have to do is pick up any other book on real estate and you'll most likely read a completely different journey to successful real estate investing. I can show you only how I accomplished my success and provide my tips and advice for you along the way.

Extraordinary in Detroit

Todd is an active real estate investor who runs one of the syndications in which I'm invested. His thoroughness and attention to detail are extremely impressive. I met with him in Cleveland, Ohio, where some of his properties are located, and he showed me how he completes his underwriting process. Along the way, I discovered that meetings like this are not normal for Todd. But a big part of why he met with me was because we had that USC connection. He graduated from there and his son attends as well. "You're a Trojan for life!"

Todd showed me his spreadsheets that evaluate every aspect of buying a property, and then we went to see them. I had earlier tried scaling my single-family investments when I started out in Beech Grove, Indiana, but my connection didn't work out, leaving me to figure out my next steps. Under Todd's guidance, I learned as much as I possibly could and bought three turnkey properties, all cash, for $300,000.

After two months, my cash flow on these three properties was excellent and I was excited and ready to double down and buy ten more properties in Ohio. It's fair to say that I was eager to scale and scale fast! That was also when I was reminded of the importance of a good, reliable team that knows how to give you advice. It was around this time that David, my financial adviser, said two of the most important words I would ever hear: *slow down.*

"Devon, I know you want to move quickly, but if you start buying a bunch of properties and then start having problems, you'll have hundreds of thousands of dollars tied into them," David told me. "Slow down and do a few at a time until you see how they perform."

Knowing what I know now, this is probably the best advice ever given to me. David taught me that it's better to tap into a market with a few properties than have something go wrong with many. Instead of taking my time, my excitement would have told me to move forward with buying several properties at once, but it would have been way too soon. I listened and I waited. Then when the time was right, I bought three more. Once I owned six properties in Ohio, I made the decision to again take my foot off the gas. I was enjoying the cash flow from these properties, but wanted to see how they would perform over the next year or two. In the meantime, I started to look at other markets where I could duplicate my process. It's called planning ahead. As months went on, I was gaining confidence in the process and knew it was finally time to scale, but I needed to scale in more than one market to make sure I diversify. One thing I have learned is people often talk about diversification, but what does that look like exactly? I find most people see it as investing in different kinds of investments such as stock market, bonds, real estate, businesses, and so on, but I have found you can pick one asset class, for me that's real estate, and diversify by investing in different sectors of that asset class, including different cities, single family homes, multifamily properties, commercial real estate, and syndications. So in this case I wanted to find another market outside of Cleveland to diversify.

I was listening to episode no. 1304 of the *BiggerPockets* podcast when Nathan Brooks was the guest. He really opened my eyes to the fact that investing in turnkey properties was a common strategy. Nathan talked on the podcast about how investing in turnkey properties was one of the easiest ways to scale your real estate investments. And at the time of this writing, his firm had bought, renovated, and sold more than five hundred houses in the past five years.

This time, instead of just listening to the podcast and taking notes, I reached out to Nathan on social media, telling him I was looking to buy properties. He agreed to meet with me in Kansas City. It might not seem like a big deal that I reached out, but it was for me. I was no longer leaning on someone else to walk me through a purchase. Up to this point, I felt like I always had someone holding my hand through the process (mostly David and Todd). This I was doing with the knowledge I've built throughout the years and connections I'd made solely on my own.

I researched the Kansas City market and did my own underwriting on which properties I found compelling and thought were a good opportunity. I gave my financial adviser a brief summary of what was going on, and when it was time, he flew out to meet Nathan with me. This trip was a *huge* confidence boost for me. After a few days of sitting down with Nathan and his team, as well as meeting the property management company that I would work with, David and I talked.

"Wow, Devon, great work!" David said to me. "Bridge Turnkey has the rehabs down pat and they are offering some good deals. I think this is something you should definitely consider moving forward with."

This is why I wanted David to come with me to Kansas City. I knew he would tell me the truth: if I was on to something I wanted his stamp of approval. Once I got that, I moved forward and purchased four single-family properties and one duplex.

In the two years I was with the Detroit Lions, I purchased a total of twelve properties—well, thirteen, actually, because, in 2019,

Some of my properties
Photo credit: Voepel Management

Camille and I bought a condo in Chandler, Arizona, for us and our soon-to-be daughter.

But in 2020, thanks to the staggering effects of COVID-19 and the uncertainties in the world, I didn't purchase any investment properties. Instead, my focus was on our wedding, taking care of my family, and making sure I continued to build the right team and infrastructure to scale my business.

In April 2020, Camille and I bought a single-family home for us in Arizona. Just like my modest apartment in New York and our modest condo in Arizona, our home was modest, too—in comparison to our earnings. While some things change as we make more money (I'll go into that soon), we decided that we didn't need a multimillion-dollar home just because we could afford one. Instead, we purchased a $1 million home fifteen minutes from where I grew up and where my parents still live to this day. Our new home was

Our home in Arizona
Photo credit: Devon Kennard

a fixer-upper, and Camille and I embarked on a big renovation to get it to our liking.

Also, as a homeowner, I didn't want to be saddled with paying a gigantic mortgage payment every month for thirty years, which would be well after I was done playing football and my NFL salary had dried up. Yes, my goal is to have more than enough mailbox money coming in (and I am close), but I would rather use that income for other things we want to do. I fully understand that not everyone is in a financial position to do this, but I took some of my money from signing with the Cardinals and put down half of the cost of the home as a down payment.

Now I was only responsible for a mortgage payment of approximately $3,000 a month. For me, that seemed reasonable. Many professional athletes have purchased expensive homes with high mortgage payments and then they are cut from the team or suffer career-ending injuries. Their incomes drop, but their mortgage payments and all the expenses associated with owning a large property (property taxes, maintenance, utilities) do not, and that is often the start of their financial troubles.

By the end of 2020, I owned fourteen doors in total (including my condo and personal home), but in 2021 I started getting itchy for more. Now it was decision-making time. Buy more in Ohio? Kansas City? Somewhere else? I did not mind expanding my portfolio in either market, but I was in Arizona playing for the Cardinals, and I really wanted to start investing in my home state.

We love living in Phoenix. Barring any crazy changes, this is where we are going to call home and raise our children. Our investment properties are in different states, but I wanted to invest in my home state, too. That was before I found out that housing prices are much higher here than in the middle of the country where I bought my other properties. I researched what landlords were charging for long-term rentals in Arizona, and I knew that after I paid off the mortgage and expenses on the property, there wasn't going to be much left. The bottom line was that I would be doing all of this work for what I figured out to be only a 4 percent or 5 percent cash-on-cash return. That just wouldn't cut it. None of the homes that Camille and I looked at seemed to give off a high enough return to buy.

When I began to get discouraged, Camille recommended that we look at houses for *short-term rentals* like Airbnb and Vrbo instead of looking at long-term rentals like I had in Ohio and Kansas City. At first, I hated this idea. It seemed like too much work, and it wasn't within my comfort zone, but then Camille found a website called AirDNA, which, for a yearly subscription, allows you to research valuable data, such as the average cost per night in a designated city and its yearly occupancy rate.

Based on this information, Camille concluded that the average per-night stay in this specific neighborhood in Tempe, Arizona, was $250, with an average occupancy of about 66 percent. I learned from Camille that it's actually a *predictable* market and you have a good idea of what you should charge; plus the AirDNA website can help you determine what your income would be. Reports have also shown that Airbnb owners can make as little as $500 a month, while others have reported $10,000 per month and more. So I based my underwriting on the fact that the average occupancy is 50 percent and the average daily rate is $225 (because I'm conservative and always factor in the worst case), but I knew that we would probably have higher occupancy.

We were pretty optimistic that if we charged more than $220 a night, we'd have more than 50 percent occupancy, so we did the math and gave all of our calculations to the lender.

With this information, I began to underwrite properties and started to find some really attractive deals, even considering the fact that prices of homes were shooting up. We bought our first Airbnb property in April 2021. All in, I spent $120,000, including the down payment, a new AC unit, new paint, and a full pool/backyard repair.

The market was so competitive that to get this property we put an offer in with an escalator up to $425K. With an escalator, anytime someone put in an offer that was higher than ours, we would immediately up our offer $1,000 until it hit the maximum of $425K. If we needed to spend a dime over $425K, we would walk away from the deal. I evaluated the numbers and chose $425K because that was the absolute highest amount I could pay for the deal and still get at least 10 percent or higher cash-on-cash (a cash-on-cash return is a rate of return that calculates the cash income earned annually on what cash I invested in the property overall). Luckily the deal went to $420K, not $425K.

So far, the Airbnb is performing well, which says a lot in the age of COVID.

The Airbnb was the only property I bought that year, but something else amazing happened. It started when one of the Ohio counties where a few of my properties were located sent me letters ordering me to fix a lead issue in a couple of my houses. Ohio homes built in the 1970s–1980s were painted with toxic lead paint. Because it was unsafe for residents, especially children, the city was mandating all investors to remedy their homes. The problem was that it would cost me $5,000 or more on each of my three properties there. A $15K expense would kill my returns for the year and, frankly, I thought it was BS. Naturally, I was pissed, so much so that I considered selling *all* of my properties in Ohio, getting my money out, and going into a different market.

My mind was pretty much made up until I told Todd about my issues and concerns, and he totally understood. Then he said, "Hey, man, you have some great properties in Ohio, and these expenses are not fun to deal with, especially when it's coming from the county. But I recommend that you at least look into refinancing your properties instead of selling."

Refinance? I agreed that I would take a look and, boy, am I glad I did. Remember, these are properties I bought all cash for $600K. So I went to the lender and found out that I could take $610K out by doing what's called a cash-out refinance loan. Those properties provided great cash flow since I purchased them and now found out I could take out all the money I invested and still keep owning the six properties that have a cash flow of about $1K a month each.

This seemed like a no-brainer, so I asked the lender to look at my Kansas City properties—four properties and one duplex that I purchased for $600K—and let me know how much I could get with a cash-out refinance. The lender told me I would get $500K.

So, in total, I bought twelve units in Ohio and KC for $1.2M and just a couple of years later I did a cash-out refinance on all of the properties, getting $1.1M back in cash. Now I only have $100K in the ground with twelve properties that generate at least $2K a month after the mortgages are paid.

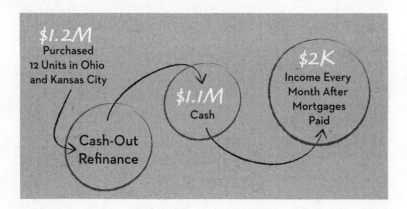

This was all possible because the value of my properties went way up.

It all adds up. Every decision I made in my real estate business led up to this massive refinance, and this single move propelled me to the next level.

Thanks to my good friend, mentor, and business partner Todd, I met the lender who allowed me to do loans on multiple properties under one loan, which is pivotal when trying to scale single-family properties.

In the next few years, my goal is to use that $1.1M I received from my cash-out to refinance and scale the amount of real estate investment properties I own. I have the infrastructure to easily handle fifty units or more, and once I get there, I will again slow down because, honestly, that's a large portfolio. I want to make sure I'm ready intellectually, with resources, relationships, and connections, to handle that much responsibility. I don't want to scale to one hundred units—or any number after that by the time you're reading this—only to find out I wasn't ready.

Now I see the power of leverage in real estate. Learning and growing changed my perspective and ultimately my investment strategy. Now I'm always moving up to the next level! I hope you do, too.

Real Estate Basics

Does my journey spark an interest in your own real estate investing path? If so, here are some tips to help you get started:

1. **Choose and evaluate the market you are interested in:** You want to look for areas that are growing or that have the potential to grow. And you want to know what the median income is in the area. What rent would you like to charge in that area? Can the residents afford that? What is the appreciation rate in that area?
2. **Find the right vendors:** such as property managers, contractors, and real estate brokers. Again this is all about making connections.
3. **Evaluating/underwriting:** You will need to learn what a good deal is and what is not. What can you afford and

what do you have to say no to? It's important to learn how to underwrite your deals. A few metrics I like to consider when underwriting a deal are the 1 percent rule, cap rate, cash-on-cash return, and appreciation potential. Once I have those four metrics, I can usually make a decision pretty quickly about whether I want to move forward with an offer or pass on that investment.

Underwriting steps:

- **1 percent rule:** When initially looking at potential investment properties, using the 1 percent rule is a quick way to see if a deal is worth considering. All you have to do is take the price of the property and multiply it by 1 percent. That gives you the amount of *rent* you should ideally be shooting for in order to make a profit. (The caveat here is the 1 percent rule is based on the market you are in. As of 2022, reaching the 1 percent rule in Arizona is challenging, so I will consider any property that meets the 0.7 percent rule). So let's say a property is $300.000: $300,000 x 1 percent = $3,000, so if I came across a property that cost $300,000 and could generate $3,000 in monthly rent, then that is definitely a property to consider buying. In this Arizona market, I use the 0.7 percent rule instead, so if I can buy a property for $300,000 then I will multiply that by 0.7 percent, which is $2,100. As long as I can rent the house out for $2,100 or more a month, I would consider buying that home.

- **Cap rate:** This is a great way to evaluate how much *income* the property actually generates. This calculation is net operating income/purchase price of the property. Net operating income means the money you bring in from renting the home minus taxes, insurance, property management, and any other operating expenses (not including mortgage payments). So let's say the NOI on a $300,000 property is $25,000. You would divide $25,000 by $300,000 which is 8.3 percent. This is a great cap rate and something I would absolutely jump on right now in this market.

- **Cash-on-cash return:** This is my favorite metric because this has a direct impact on my mailbox money. The formula is this: net income after financing (NIAF)/capital invested. NIAF means you take the NOI and subtract the mortgage payments. What is left is the net income after financing. You take that number and divide it by how much money you originally invested in the deal. So let's say your NIAF is $7,500 and to purchase the $300,000 property you put 25 percent down, which is $75,000. That means you would take $7,500 and divide it by $75,000, which gives you a 10 percent return. For me, any deal that I can get an 8 percent COC return or higher on is one I will definitely buy!

- **Appreciation Potential:** This is the one evaluation I consider that is actually based on *speculation*. When I am evaluating a potential area in which to invest, I like to look at the appreciation rate over the last five years in that area and get a sense of how much and how fast properties in the area are appreciating. I typically like to find areas where properties are appreciating at 3 percent or higher annually. What's important here is *passive appreciation*, meaning you buy the property and do

nothing to it, but it increases in value every year by
3 percent or greater. You can also get appreciation for a
property by getting a deal on a property that is below
market value. For instance, if I buy a property for
$300,000 but most of the similar properties in the
neighborhood are selling for $330,000, then I
automatically have built-in equity as soon as I purchase
the property. The last way to get appreciation is by
forcing it. You can force appreciation by buying a
property for $300,000 putting $20,000 of work into the
house to make it look nicer, and then knowing that the
new renovations will push the value of the property to
$350,000 or more. This is called *forced appreciation*
because you are doing something to the property to
increase its value.

4. **Consider buying turnkey properties:** These take little
   to no repair work once you buy them. If you are just
   starting out, know little about real estate, or you're too
   busy to put a lot of time into it, a property that's ready
   to go is easier than a fixer-upper. The downside is your
   return might not be as high, at least initially, but
   depending on your goals and lifestyle, that is okay—at
   least it is for me.

5. **Consider flipping homes:** If you're someone who has a
   little more risk tolerance and is willing to put in manual labor, flipping a home is a great way to generate a
   good return in a short amount of time.

6. **Consider investing out of state:** Many people are
   afraid to invest where they don't live, but it's a great

way to get into the game. If I had to buy my first property in Phoenix, I don't know if and when I would have
gotten into real estate because it was so much more
expensive. But in the Midwest, the average price was
$100,000, putting me in a position to buy affordably.
You can find a real estate deal anywhere, but keep in
mind that those deals are going to look different
depending on where you are buying property.

7. **Consider buying multifamily properties:** Consider
this: you purchase a multifamily home with *four* units
and rent each out for $1,000 a month. Let's say that one
month, someone defaults on their payment, but you
still have $3,000 coming in from the other tenants.
Now, if you buy a single home and rent it out for
$2,000 a month and that renter defaults, you're out the
entire amount. There are some perks to multifamily. In
addition, multifamily investments allow you to scale
faster.

8. **Consider owning triple net lease commercial buildings:** *Triple net* (or NNN) means that the tenant is covering all the property expenses: usually property taxes,
insurance, and maintenance. As the owner, you do not
have to worry about any of the expenses involving the
property. If you purchase an NNN lease property, all
you need to deduct from your income is the loan payment. NNN lease investments are truly passive and justify why I will eventually invest in this kind of
commercial property as well. The key with NNN lease
properties is finding tenants with very strong finances.
If you can manage to buy a building with a tenant that

is a national brand like McDonald's, Starbucks, Amazon, or Panera, then you are in great shape. One thing to note is the more established the tenant, typically the lower the return you can expect, which is why some people buy NNN leases with tenants that are not as established as major national companies because although it's riskier their return is higher.

You might be willing to take even more risks than I have taken or scale faster than I did. If I wasn't so risk averse, I would have an even larger portfolio, but it boils down to the reality that I never want to lose my money, so I'm super conservative.

Get ready to blaze your own trails.

 Buying real estate will help you flip the bag! There are so many ways to invest in real estate, so find which strategy matches your risk tolerance and personality and go for it!

CHAPTER THIRTEEN

Next-Level Investing: Real Estate Syndications

Don't be afraid to give up the good to go for the great.
—John D. Rockefeller

Everyone starts their financial journey somewhere, right? And the only place to go from wherever you are now is up, even if you're starting from zero. The more your wealth then builds, the more financial opportunities will open up for you. For me, I was fortunate to build enough wealth early on in my NFL career to become what's called an *accredited investor*. It's a very important step on my own financial journey and one that opened the door to profitable investments in real estate syndications.

Let me explain how I got here and, yes, how you can, too. Ever since I bought my first investment property, I went from being pretty interested in the real estate industry to becoming absolutely absorbed in it and wanting to make it my primary focus outside football. By owning real estate, I not only love the fact that I am making a lot of mailbox money, but I am also providing places to live for people who need them—it's a win-win situation.

But as much as I love owning all of these properties, I am not a put-all-my-eggs-in-one-basket kind of guy. Owning a property takes a lot of work, but I realized that sometimes I just want the benefits of investing in real estate without having to be responsible for the physical property.

Investing in a *real estate syndication* gives me the best of both worlds. I can partially own property and reap the benefits, but I'm not the one who worries about paying the mortgage or repairing the roof.

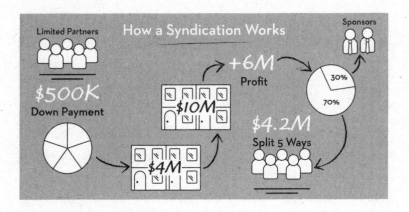

If you're confused about how investing in a syndication works, here is an easy-to-understand example. Let's say that a friend of yours and his partners (who are all typically called the sponsors or general partners in syndications) are trying to buy a fourplex—a building that would house four separate families under one roof. The cost of the fourplex is $4 million, but the sponsors don't have enough resources or don't want to tie up all of their own money in this investment, so your friend approaches you and others and asks all of you to invest with him and his partners on the deal.

"We are trying to buy this property and need $500,000 for a down payment and remodeling. Would you like to invest with me?" he says. "We can sign a contract that outlines the relationship and the payment structure. You can be a silent partner where I do all of the work and you just put in the capital."

In a real estate syndication deal, investors (in this example that would be you and whoever else your friend got to agree to invest in the deal) pool their money to buy a piece of property that the sponsors/GPs could not or did not want to purchase on their own. Depending on the deal, there can be one or several GPs. Then there can be anywhere from a handful of investors or hundreds of investors (who are often called limited partners or LPs). The GPs who purchase the property are the ones who pay the mortgage and all the expenses as well as deal with the day-to-day operations. GPs typically invest anywhere from 5 to 20 percent of the total required equity capital. LPs cover the rest.

LPs are guaranteed a preferred rate of return that they will receive no matter what, as long as the deal succeeds. In most of the syndications I am in, the preferred return is paid out quarterly. Let's say I'm the one who invests $100K into a deal and have a preferred return of 8 percent based on the contract with the GPs. I will receive $2,000 every three months until that real estate deal is sold.

Tip: I will not become an investor in a
syndication deal unless there's a preferred rate
of return of at least 7 percent or higher.

After all the expenses are paid and before the GPs pay themselves, the LPs are given their share.

On top of that preferred return, the LPs also earn money from the sale or refinance of the property. In many of the syndications I am in, once the property is sold or refinanced, all the LPs earn a 70/30 split of that excess capital. For example, let's say I was one of the five friends who invested $100K each as an LP in that $4M fourplex example that I mentioned earlier, for a total of $500K. In addition to that $8K a year for five years straight off of that investment, I also receive a portion of the profit when the property is sold.

So, let's say that the GPs get an offer from a buyer of $10M, or $6M more than they originally bought it for five years ago. That is a good profitable deal, so the GPs decide to sell. According to the agreement that the LPs signed, once a sale happens the LPs split the profit with the GPs 70/30. So that means that the LPs will receive 70 percent of the $6M, which is $4.2M. Since there are five LPs in this deal, $4.2M split five ways is $840K each.

So in this mock deal, I am an LP, a silent investor who put in $100K and received a total of $40K in preferred returns over five years ($8K a year × five years). Then after the sale, I also received my portion of the proceeds or $840K. For me, investing in a deal like this is a *no brainer*!

Based on the example above, you may ask, "What is in it for the GPs?" Well, rest assured the GPs typically make even more money than the LPs do in most syndications, and in most cases, the GPs are not even putting a large portion of their own money into the deals.

So to keep things simple, let's say in the fourplex example above there was only one GP and he put $50K of his own money into the deal. He would still receive the preferred return so he will make $4K annually off his $50K investment. Additionally, syndications have fees baked into the deals. There could be a 1 percent acquisition fee, which means that as soon as the property is officially acquired, the GP receives a payment of 1 percent based on the purchase price of the property. So 1 percent of a $4M purchase price is $40K, so just by securing the property, the GP is getting the majority of his initial $50K investment back.

———

Tip: I do not invest in any syndication where the GPs haven't invested at least some of their own capital. I like to know they have legitimate financial skin in the game.

———

Other fees that we won't dive into but you shouldn't be surprised to see are disposition fees, loan origination fees, and management fees, just to name a few.

So the GP would receive $40K in fees, $20K in his preferred return over the course of five years, *and* his 30 percent of the 70/30 split with the LPs. Then, if the property sells for $10M, this GP will receive an additional $3M. This is why you should *not* feel bad for the GPs. Even though they are carrying the burden of acquiring and managing their real estate deal, they are poised to benefit greatly financially.

Investing in a real estate syndication is advantageous for a variety of reasons. The first is that I can't be everywhere at once, so investing in real estate on paper versus physical properties is good for my lifestyle. I'm also admittedly not an expert on all the different types of real estate. I leave it up to the experts to know their particular market and find the best investment-worthy properties.

All I am concerned with is studying the syndication's financial information and underwriting before I make a final decision to invest or not. By doing this, I have invested in syndications for single-family homes, apartment complexes, medical buildings, senior living centers, hotels, and storage units, to name a few, just by sitting at home.

Next, compared to the physical properties that I actually own, when I am adding a physical property to my personal investment portfolio, I am putting it in my name or in the name of my business with me as the guarantor, which makes me liable for that property. This isn't the case with syndications. My name is not on the mortgage or title documents of a syndicated property. Therefore, I limit my risk potential. In the fourplex example, all I have risked is my $100,000 investment and nothing more because the property isn't in my name.

My personal investment portfolio has now become very diversified, which is exactly what I was looking to do. In 2015 I purchased my first physical property. Now my portfolio looks like this:

- Thirty-two syndications
- Six units in Cleveland, Ohio
- Six units in Kansas City, Missouri
- Four units in Memphis, Tennessee
- Four units in Phoenix, Arizona, with intent to expand this portfolio exponentially over the next few years.

I am hoping you follow a similar path as you build your own wealth. My real estate syndications are earning hundreds of thousands of dollars every year in mailbox money for me through a combination of monthly and annual dividend payments (through

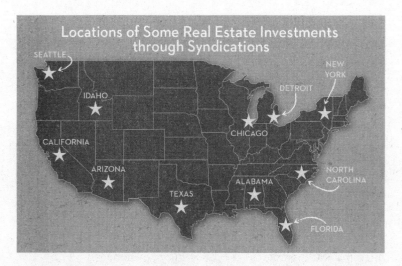

preferred returns) as well as the appreciation and growth of the properties that the syndications own. Syndications provide instant mailbox money in a very conservative way. This works for me because, like I keep saying, I do not have a high-risk tolerance.

Money-Back Not Guaranteed

What if the syndication isn't performing positively? Can you withdraw your investment? It depends.

Every investment comes with its own pros and cons and contingencies that are outlined before you invest, but typically your investment is not liquid. That is, you can't withdraw it at any time unless there is some kind of special provision already established in your agreement. For example, the syndication might include a hardship provision, so in case of a divorce, serious illness, or death, the money can be withdrawn.

If I invest in a syndication, I typically intend to hold that money for the entirety of the fund, which should also be outlined in the financial documents. If you are ever in a situation where you really want your money out, it does not hurt to ask the GP because he or she might be willing to let you out as long as they have someone else who can replace your capital. Remember that all investments come with risks, so be sure that you and key members of your team (attorney, financial person for starters) read the fine print.

You Need to Be an Accredited Investor

Earlier, I mentioned that I finally achieved the level of *accredited investor*. That's important because it's the one requirement to participate in an SEC-backed real estate syndication.

According to the SEC, to become an accredited investor, you must meet at least one of the following requirements:

- $1 million net worth individually or jointly,
- $200,000 or higher annual income ($300,000 joint income) for the last two years with the expectation to earn at least that this year, or
- having professional knowledge, experience, or certifications.

According to my financial adviser, David, the syndication is protecting itself by bringing in only accredited investors. "Investors have to be vetted by an adviser," he said.

If you're fortunate to be at a point in your life where you meet at least one of the accredited investor qualifications, consider real estate syndications. This is a common way for high-wealth individuals to build generational wealth.

And if you aren't a high-wealth individual yet, don't worry. The steps are in place for you to get there. You have something to strive for and options to consider when you arrive.

How Can You Find Real Estate Syndications?

Google: Google is the easiest way to look for potential deals. Search "real estate syndications," or narrow it down to specific markets—for example, "real estate syndications in Phoenix, Arizona," and see what comes up. The majority of syndications have portals that their clients and potential investors can access.

Network: If you have friends, family, or associates who are accredited investors, ask them if they are invested in any real estate syndications or if they plan to. It's likely they really believe in it and did some underwriting of their own before choosing to invest. Also, once you start meeting and connecting with people in the real estate space, you will be surprised by the opportunities that come your way. I have built relationships with people in Detroit that led me to invest. This was true after I joined the Cardinals. I think finding great GPs is key, because once you find someone who really knows what they are doing and that you can trust, you invest in their deals over and over again.

Podcasts: Listen up. By listening to top real estate podcasts, you get a detailed understanding of syndications and access to some very capable syndicators. Brandon Turner of the *BiggerPockets* podcast has his own syndication deal, and he and cohost David Greene often interview real estate investors who are GPs and own their own funds. *The Real Wealth Show* podcast host Kathy Fettke is also a syndicator.

I've said before that my journey to building wealth and achieving my own American dream is going to look different than yours. I started with purchasing physical properties and then jumped into syndications. You might jump straight into syndications and then own physical properties, or you might invest in one but not the other.

In my opinion, I believe it's beneficial to do both at some point. The combination of investments has provided me with diversification and has helped me to surpass my financial goals. I do not think I would have as much cash flow and mailbox money as I do if I had just invested in physical properties, especially while I am still playing in the NFL.

Want to Invest in Real Estate Syndications?

1. **Evaluate:** Make sure you're investing in deals that make sense. Remember my golden rule: if you can't understand and explain the investment, you shouldn't be part of it.

2. **Research:** Check the GP's track record. Have they had success building syndications? How did their previous syndication perform?

3. **Figure out fees:** One thing that a lot of skeptical syndications have in common is that the fee structure is too high. There are reasonable fees to expect—acquisition fees, disposition fees, loan origination fees, and management fees, just to name a few. If the percentage is getting so high that the GPs are making a killing before they even deliver on their promises, that is usually a deal I stay away from. I advise you to do the same!

4. **Check the underwriting:** What kind of return are the GPs expecting, and are their projections aggressive or conservative? When I was first starting out, I would ask other mentors of mine to review any syndication I was looking at and give me feedback. I would take notes on their responses and study that. After a while, you begin to see the trends and know the right things to look at

and ask for. I'm a conservative investor, so if the numbers ever look too good to be true, that is usually a red flag for me, and I typically won't invest.

Beware!

"You can invest as little as $10 in a real estate syndication and make tons of money!" Maybe you've seen this on an infomercial or in an ad online. I am aware that there are crowdfunding sites for real estate deals, but truth be told, I know nothing about them. I have never invested in something that wasn't SEC-protected, so if you're interested in pursuing this kind of syndication investment, make sure you perform your due diligence on the platform and read your contracts closely, but do not invest if something doesn't look or feel right. Trust your gut, which gets fine-tuned by experience.

Bad Apples

Like any investment opportunity, there are bad apples trying to rip off people.

"When you make as much money as, say, a professional athlete or successful entrepreneur, you will get many investment opportunities thrown at you. But so many people do not understand what they are reading," David said. "It becomes work, and many people do not take the steps to understand any of it."

Don't fall into this category. This is why improving your *financial literacy* is important. As you learn more, there is less chance that you'll be taken advantage of because you'll know what doesn't sound right to you.

I like to compare learning about real estate syndications to learning a football playbook. If you have never seen a football playbook before, it would look extremely complicated. You would see a bunch of letters and lines that probably mean little to nothing to you. Once you have the basics down, you can then look at a defensive play for a few seconds and have a good idea of what you are looking at. Syndications are no different; you just need the reps of looking at and analyzing them, so take the time to learn about them. Before you know it, you'll be vetting and investing in syndications with ease.

It all adds up.

My career feels different now that I've built my financial wealth. Now I'm doing it because I love the game. It's what I *want* to do, not what I *have* to do. I've also gotten to the point in my life where if my football career comes to an end, I'm financially stable to do whatever I want to do next.

 Almost every wealthy person I know has invested in a syndication of some form. I think that's the case because it's an effective way to make sure your money is working for you while you sleep and can play a major role in helping you flip the bag in your life!

CHAPTER FOURTEEN

A Financial Touchdown!

I'm more interested in what I'm about to do
than what I've already done.

TOUCHDOWN

Become an HS All-American

10 · 10

Choose USC

20 · 20

Network and leverage USC for two degrees

30 · 30

Become one of a small list of players to graduate
with two degrees before getting drafted

40

40

Start as a rookie and buy a
first investment property

50

50

Meet David, start investing in syndications

40

40

Sign with Detroit Lions

30

30

Meet Todd, start investing in Ohio

20

20

Walter Payton Man of the Year
Award finalist and team captain

10

10

TOUCHDOWN

CHAPTER FIFTEEN

True Living Comes from Giving

We make a living by what we get,
but we make a life by what we give.
—Winston Churchill

I want to have a heart like Jimsen's.

The young Haitian boy was approximately ten to twelve years old and spoke broken English, but he seemed to understand everything I said. Due to the tragic earthquakes that hit that region in 2010, he had been through more tragedy and heartache than any child should endure.

I was in Haiti for five days on a mission trip with eleven other USC students, including my teammate, Matt Barkley, and his parents, who had organized it. We were there to build four homes for four families in the area where Jimsen lived. He just seemed to gravitate to me, eager to help. Jimsen lived in an area where residents walked miles just to get water. It wasn't even clean water, which meant they could get sick or worse from it. A thin tarp tent held up by sticks was their temporary home, their only barrier to the harsh elements.

Being in Haiti was one of the most humbling experiences of my life.

On the last day of our trip, we were told that if there was anything we wanted to give to the kids, especially leftover food, they would be more than happy to take it.

My last snack bar would be perfect, I thought to myself.

I knew it would be the first, and probably the last, time that Jimsen would eat that day. I expected him to tear it open and devour it, but he broke off several pieces and walked over to his younger brother and sister. Instead of keeping an entire bar for himself, Jimsen shared it and ended up enjoying one small bite. He thought of his siblings before he thought of himself.

I was touched, of course . . . and changed. In the years since, when I felt I had cause to be bitter or angry about some life

Me, Jimsen, and his friends
Photo credit: Devon Kennard

circumstance, maybe believing I wasn't living my best life, I think of Jimsen, who is probably still struggling to find meals for himself and his siblings.

I want to have a heart like Jimsen's.

Earthquakes

Here's what happened where Jimsen lived: In 2010, a catastrophic 7.0 earthquake struck Haiti, the third-largest country in the Caribbean. The devastation left behind was gut-wrenching, killing almost two hundred thousand people and destroying homes and properties. Looking around, I let it soak in how brutal the conditions were that Jimsen lived in, and I was deeply saddened by the poverty. It was a truly heartbreaking yet eye-opening experience that I will never forget.

Honestly, I have trained hard for everything I've accomplished so far in my career, but it was nothing compared to the amount of physical work it took to build those four homes in Haiti. To this day, they were some of the hardest and longest days of manual labor I've ever had in my life, yet perhaps the most satisfying to me for the significance of what we are able to accomplish for others in great need.

In high school, I worked for an after-school program—my first paying job—helping kids with their homework and playing outside with them before their parents came to pick them up. During my time at USC, I volunteered to go to Skid Row in Los Angeles around the holidays and hand out food and gifts to kids. In those days I was also an eager volunteer for visiting the sick kids at local hospitals. Doing all of this reaffirmed in me that working with kids is a passion of mine.

The mission's trip to Haiti gave me perspective about my own blessings, and it solidified the fact for me that if/when I got to the NFL, I would continue to work with youth.

Soon after my dad retired from the NFL, he started a group home in Phoenix, Arizona, where he helped give troubled kids a second chance by providing a safe environment for them in which to grow up. He also founded the DK Foundation, a nonprofit organization to help the community of Stockton, California. I was impressed that my dad returned to the area where he grew up to help his community, and I took notice that so much of what he did involved giving back to kids. He held youth football camps that I participated in as a youngster. He held lollipop races, for which the fastest player would get a trophy. Pros such as Michael Irvin, one of his Dallas Cowboy teammates, came out to watch. Dad never really talked about charity work or tried to persuade me to get involved, but he didn't have to. I saw firsthand the impact he had on kids, and I knew that giving back would become an important part of my life as well.

Just so you know, as much as you see NFL players doing charity work, it might surprise you to know that it is not a requirement. If you see an NFL player donating his time or his money, it's all from his own heart.

When I was still in college going for my second degree, I was required to write a thesis for my master's degree. I wrote mine on starting my own nonprofit. My vision was first to revitalize my dad's old nonprofit, DK Foundation, but after further research, I realized the amount of time and money that went into starting a nonprofit. Then I also saw that so many athletes were starting their own foundations, but very few of them were making a great impact. So I made the decision to identify those organizations that already had everything figured out and work with them. It was effective and made the most sense to me. There are start-up costs to running a nonprofit organization, and then you have to keep raising money. It's a process that you need to be committed to, and that's why many fail. On the other hand, working with a successful organization that you can help bring awareness, attention, and impact to seems like a much better option.

At the time, I had just gotten drafted into the NFL and was trying to kick-start my investment portfolio, and running a nonprofit was like having another job. As a result, putting my time, money, and resources into an already-established organization was the best decision for me. That is still my approach today.

Help for New City Kids

My life has always been about more than just making as much money as I can. It's also been about giving back and teaching as much as I know. I've said it before and I'll say it again—I'm not the smartest guy in the room, but I don't want to wait to share what I've learned so far until I have it all figured out. If I did that, I would never get to the "finish line" and therefore would not ever be sharing what I do know at the time.

When I was with the New York Giants, I volunteered with New City Kids in Jersey City, an after-school program where kids from elementary up to high school are tutored and taught to play instruments such as the piano and drums. What I loved about New City Kids is they empowered the older high school kids, too, by hiring some as tutors for the younger elementary school kids. The caveat was that the older kids had to show proof of great attendance at school and maintain a 3.0 GPA. As long as you met

At New City Kids
Photo credit: Devon Kennard

the requirements, you could be hired. This was good for the young kids, as well, because it gave them someone in their own neighborhood to look up to!

I went there as often as I could on my off days and in the off-season. I fell in love with their program and admired the success and impact they were having in the community. My involvement and endorsement of New City Kids led to the Giants donating $20,000 to the organization.

Then I started #ReadingwithDK. My mission? To make reading cool again for all ages. Hearing a teacher talking about how cool reading is, is one thing, but having professional athletes deliver that same message can have a more robust impact. Seeing someone like Cowboys quarterback Dak Prescott reading on his off day is effective, and that's exactly what I wanted to do.

Once I arrived in Detroit, I was introduced to the Midnight Golf Program, another after-school program that focuses on mentorship and guidance for high school seniors. Students apply to get in because the demand is so high. Once the students are accepted, they learn valuable skills that include SAT and ACT test prep, how to apply for colleges, and how to deal with time management once they enter college.

With scholarship recipients from the Midnight Golf Program
Photo credit: Devon Kennard

All of these skills are essential for these students' success, and the mentorship sets them up to achieve their goals. Most of these kids will be first-generation college students with no guidance on what the process to get into college could/should look like. That's where Midnight Golf came in. Kids who worked hard and had good grades were losing out on opportunities to go to college simply because they couldn't afford it. This is a real tragedy in underserved communities. Midnight Golf was life altering and life saving for many of the kids I met.

With my growing financial resources, I felt that it was time to create the Devon Kennard Scholarship Fund in 2018, specifically for the Midnight Golf Program students. The requirements for my scholarship were that each student had to send me their transcripts, college acceptance letters, and their own letter to me telling me about a book they had read and the impact it had had on their life. In the first year of the fund, I had fifty applicants and gave out two scholarships. The kids didn't make it easy. There were so many deserving students. I still follow on social media the kids who won my award, and I get in touch with them from time to time.

I also joined the Detroit Lions' leadership council, which identified nonprofit organizations in the greater Detroit area that were of particular interest to them because of that nonprofit's demonstrated passion in fulfilling their mission, and for that the council wanted to help make a difference. The council elected a handful of organizations that they chose to work with and then raised over a million dollars in two years to donate to these organizations.

I've never been the type of guy who just wants to give a monetary donation. Monetary donations are great, and I don't minimize the impact they have on organizations, but I want to be hands on with anything I do. With that in mind, I made sure that the council hosted a variety of community events to help raise money and awareness as well.

Both 2018 and 2019 were pivotal years in this country when it came to social injustices—specifically, the hate crime murder of

25-year-old Ahmaud Arbery in Georgia while he was jogging, as well as several other tragedies involving African Americans taken from us too soon. I was proud to be a part of a group of teammates really trying to make a difference in a city like Detroit.

Fast-forward to Arizona, where I decided to devote my time and energy to ICAN, a free after-school program that serves East Valley youth. Its mission is to provide free, comprehensive programs that empower youth to be productive, self-confident, and responsible members of the community. ICAN's goal is to break the cycle of poverty, creating a new pathway for youth to achieve future success. This program matched my goals of working with kids, and I was excited to be giving back to this close-to-home organization. I sent a text to my dad telling him all about it.

"Wow, that's crazy!" he replied.

"Why?"

"When I signed with the Arizona Cardinals, I worked with that organization, too!"

That connection to my dad was so cool because it happened organically. I saw the impact on the kids he helped throughout his career, and I wanted to have that same impact. I wanted to change lives because, ultimately, my dad did that for me too.

In my years with the Cardinals (so far), I have wanted to do more in the area of community involvement, but the presence of COVID-19 has slowed down things. Luckily, we are starting to build momentum again, and I'm excited about that because it's in my own hometown.

Financial literacy is extremely important to me as well. I am working with an organization called World of Money, which brings kids from all over the country to New York for courses on financial literacy. I became part of their national advisory council in 2021 because I strongly felt that they had a curriculum that needed to be spread to all kids across the country. I think financial education for our youth, especially in underserved communities, can be the catalyst to positive change for so many things in this country. I have been blessed with the passion and desire to leave my mark when it comes to teaching and encouraging people of all ages, backgrounds, and ethnicities to take financial literacy seriously.

With kids at ICAN
Photo credit: Devon Kennard

I have stayed focused and committed to my game plan to work with kids and have made decent headway on achieving just that. Yet, I believe my best work is ahead of me.

Find the Time

As you are working toward your goals and your definition of the American dream, you should find time to give back in some capacity that works for you, no matter how small.

Do something. Do anything. *It all adds up.*

I understand that time is short for you as you're committed to your work and your family. But time is also of the essence with others who need your help, your expertise, and your guidance. Please be sensitive to that in others in their time of great need. During the season, I spend my off days and some of my free time volunteering, while I continue to balance being a father of two young children, a husband, an investor, and an NFL player.

Bring Someone with You

Not sure where to start? If you want to change the world, start at home. Before I try to have a positive impact on anybody else, I want to have a positive impact on my wife and kids.

When Camille and I first met, she was making good money managing a dental office. Her own career plan was to save some money and go to dental school so she could become a dentist. Her mother is in the dental field, too, and it was something Camille had always wanted to do.

She was working long days and then taking online classes after work to finish her undergrad degree. She doesn't shy away from work, and I love and respect her for that, but once we were together, she started to learn about mailbox money, too.

Early in our relationship, we had a deeper conversation about her interests and dreams and our (future) children. Camille realized that becoming a dentist would mean long hours away from the kids and accumulating even more debt. With this realization in mind, our discussions shifted into other options for her professionally that would not require going to dental school, such as owning a dental office and renting the space out to dentists. After a few years of being a sounding board for me at home, Camille also gained a genuine interest for real estate; so after we got married, she chose to get her real estate license. Today, she's working with one of the best real estate groups in Arizona. She's also adding value to what I'm doing with real estate investments. That's what it means to bring someone with you or help someone get in a position to succeed. I want to bring as many people with me as I can, and you should, too.

Do you have kids? Let them see your work ethic. I can tell you firsthand that kids listen to half of what you say but watch everything you do! Instill habits in them to help them achieve their goals. There are days my daughter doesn't want to go to gymnastics or ballet, so we teach her that when you make a commitment, you need to stick to it. I make sure that I set that example so my girls can see what that looks like. Those messages have made an impact on her. So don't let yourself off the hook by saying you are too busy. The least you can do is make an impact at home and in your direct sphere of influence—family, friends, coworkers.

Then, once you have more time, extend your reach into the community and the rest of the world. Making an impact is an evolution that grows as you and your financial wealth grow. Share your knowledge, gifts, and talents with the world, especially with those who don't have access to them.

And don't forget to have a heart like Jimsen's.

The unspoken rule for me when it comes to flipping the bag is that once you have done it, you must teach someone else to do it, too! People will forget what you did but will forever remember how you made them feel, so leave people with a sense of empowerment by spreading what you've learned in this book and how you have applied it to your own life! The world needs to hear *your* story!

ACKNOWLEDGMENTS

Writing this book was more difficult than I ever imagined. I would not have been able to do it without the best team in the world around me:

My wife, Camille: Thank you for your patience with me and willingness to accept the late nights and early mornings as I typed away and read segments out loud. Your feedback and support along the way meant the world to me.

My daughters, Camryn and Carsyn: You two are my inspiration and motivation in everything I do, including this book. I hope I have given you something to build upon. Daddy loves you both! Thank you!

Vanessa Haynes: Thank you for helping me find my voice and giving me the confidence I needed to pursue writing this book in the first place. Writing this book was a lifelong dream of mine, and you fanned the flames to make it happen. Thank you!

Lisa Iannucci: This book would not have been possible without your consistent direction, feedback, and thoroughness throughout the process. I will never forget the sacrifices you made to help me get this book across the finish line. Thank you!

David Johan: Everything I have written in this book originated from conversations you and I have had dating back to 2015. My knowledge and understanding of personal finance would not be where it is today without your commitment and patience in teaching me. Thank you!

To Todd, Kyle, Stuart, Mike, Nathan, and Erik: You all have played a major role in my financial and investment journey so far, and I thank you for your mentorship and friendship. I would not have a story to tell if it wasn't for meeting and working with you all. Thank you!

APPENDIX: RESOURCES

Udemy: I downloaded the Udemy app and took lessons on creating Excel spreadsheets. I was never taught how to use Excel properly, so this was a big help. I learned how to build my own spreadsheets for my personal expense reports and for breaking down income and expenses in any of my business dealings; https://www.udemy.com/.

Mint: When I first started taking care of my money, I took advantage of apps such as Mint to plug in my bank accounts and get a real-time breakdown of my monthly earnings and spending; https://mint.intuit.com.

Real Estate and Financial Independence: Chad "Coach" Carson gives concrete, actionable steps through his podcast, webinars, and other resources that are extremely beneficial to get you into real estate; https://www.coachcarson.com.

Graham Stephan: Graham skipped college and pursued real estate sales when he was eighteen. By the time he was twenty-six, he was a millionaire. His YouTube channel walks you through his successes, obstacles, and sacrifices, and he gives great personal finance advice; https://www.youtube.com/c/GrahamStephan.

Thach Nguyen: Thach is a Vietnamese refugee who once lived in a homeless shelter. He has been a real estate agent with Windermere Real Estate in Seattle, Washington, since 1991 and offers courses as well as really helpful real estate tips and suggestions on his social media; https://www.instagram.com/thachnguyen.

GQ Sports: With GQ Sports, you get an all-access look into how athletes shop, train, travel, and showcase their love of style, menswear, and sneakers; http://youtube.com/c/Gqsports.

BiggerPockets **Podcast and Resources:** https://www.biggerpockets.com/.

Earn Your Leisure Podcast: Hosted by Rashad Bilal and Troy Millings, this podcast provides behind-the-scenes financial views into the entertainment and sports industries as well as highlights back stories of entrepreneurs. They also host events, including their Investfest, an in-person experience that combines investing, entrepreneurship, pop culture, and entertainment in a festival setting; https://www.earnyourleisure.com.

Books

Rich Dad Poor Dad: What the Rich Teach Their Kids About Money—That the Poor and Middle Class Do Not! by Robert T. Kiyosaki

Money: Master the Game: 7 Simple Steps to Financial Freedom by Tony Robbins, Jeremy Bobb

The Perfect Day to Boss Up: A Hustler's Guide to Building Your Empire by Rick Ross, Neil Martinez-Belkin

I Can't Make This Up: Life Lessons by Kevin Hart

Shoe Dog: A Memoir by the Creator of Nike, Phil Knight

NOTES

Chapter 1

1. John Keim, "With Average NFL Career 3.3 years, Players Motivated to Complete MBA Program," ESPN.com, July 29, 2016, https://www.espn.com/blog/nflnation/post/_/id/207780/current-and-former-nfl-players-in-the-drivers-seat-after-completing-mba-program.

2. US Census Bureau, "Figure 3: Distribution of Total Population and Poverty by Race Using the Official Poverty Measure: 2021," September 13, 2022, https://www.census.gov/content/dam/Census/library/visualizations/2022/demo/p60-277/figure3.pdf.

Chapter 3

1. Melanie Hanson, "Student Loan Default Rate," Education Data Initiative, updated December 19, 2021, https://educationdata.org/student-loan-default-rate.

2. "Demographics of Debt," Debt.org, updated February 23, 2022, https://www.debt.org/faqs/americans-in-debt/demographics/.

3. Christian E. Weller and Lily Roberts, "Eliminating the Black-White Wealth Gap Is a Generational Challenge," Center for American Progress, March 19, 2021, https://www.americanprogress.org/article/eliminating-black-white-wealth-gap-generational-challenge/.

4. Olugbenga Ajilore, "On the Persistence of the Black-White Unemployment Gap," Center for American Progress, February 24, 2020, https://www.americanprogress.org/article/persistence-black-white-unemployment-gap/.

5. Dedrick Asante-Muhammad, Jamie Buell, and Joshua Devine, "60% Black Homeownership: A Radical Goal for Black Wealth Development," National Community Reinvestment Coalition, March 2, 2021, https://ncrc.org/60-black-homeownership-a-radical-goal-for-black-wealth-development/.

6. "Longstanding Disparity Between Black and White Investors Narrows, but New Risks Emerge," Yahoo Business Wire, April 5, 2022, https://www

.yahoo.com/now/longstanding-disparity-between-black-white-120000146
.html.

7. Olugbenga Ajilore, "The Persistent Black-White Unemployment Gap Is
Built into the Labor Market," Center for American Progress, September 28,
2020, https://www.americanprogress.org/article/persistent-black-white
-unemployment-gap-built-labor-market/.

Chapter 4

1. "Welcome to the Financial Personality Quiz," Marcus: by Goldman Sachs,
January 26, 2021, https://www.marcus.com/us/en/resources/lifestyle
/discover-your-financial-personality.

Chapter 6

1. "Benefits of Self-Affirmation," Carnegie Mellon University, n.d., https://
www.cmu.edu/homepage/health/2013/summer/benefits-of-self-affirmation
.shtml.

Chapter 7

1. Although he recently sold his majority stakes in March 2021.

INDEX

ABOUT THE AUTHOR

It didn't take long for NFL linebacker Devon Kennard to realize football wasn't going to last forever.

Over the last decade, Kennard, who recently turned 31, has developed into a savvy real estate investor, amassing a multimillion-dollar portfolio that he says has averaged an impressive 8 percent to 12 percent return. By funneling his time, effort, and money into ensuring he never becomes another statistic, Kennard has obtained the financial security and independence he so adamantly sought and has effectively taken control of his family's financial future.

For now, Kennard is maintaining his financial strategies while focusing on his on-field play. He's succeeded in a way many other players have not, securing his future and preserving the generational wealth he has accumulated while playing football. Football isn't going to last forever, and when it does come to an end, Kennard will be ready.